Kevin Keegan

Kevin Keegan

An Intimate Portrait of Football's Last Romantic

Ian Ridley

SIMON & SCHUSTER

London · New York · Sydney · Toronto

A CBS COMPANY

First published in Great Britain in 2008 by Simon & Schuster UK Ltd
A CBS COMPANY

1 3 5 7 9 10 8 6 4 2

Simon & Schuster UK Ltd
1st Floor
222 Gray's Inn Road
London
WC1X 8HB

www.simonsays.co.uk

Simon & Schuster Australia
Sydney

PICTURE CREDITS
PA Photos: 1, 3, 4, 5, 6, 7, 8, 9, 11, 13, 17, 18, 19, 20, 22
Getty Images: 2, 14, 21
Mirrorpix: 10, 15, 16
National Archives: 12

A CIP catalogue for this book is available
from the British Library.

ISBN: 978-1-84737-378-6

Typeset in Palatino by MRules
Printed in the UK by CPI Mackays, Chatham ME5 8TD

CONTENTS

ACKNOWLEDGEMENTS

My thanks go first to a person who has not helped me with this project: the book's subject, Kevin Keegan. His has been a fascinating life in football for the last forty or so years and he is a compelling subject.

'Biography,' Thomas Carlyle once wrote, 'is the only true history.' While I cannot make such grandiose claims about this portrait of Keegan, I do hope that it is a fair, accurate and entertaining account of the many highs and fewer lows of his career. It is also my wish to recount a great change in the English game and its place in our culture over five decades' – change which Keegan himself mirrors.

I did not seek to gain Keegan's co-operation when writing this book, not simply because his autobiography has already told his story from his own point of view. I did not want to be beholden to anything but the story as I see it; I wanted to hear testimony from people who have been close to Keegan without them feeling under any undue obligation. I am grateful to all those who have given of their time and experience to help produce this portrait.

Thanks to Sir Bobby Robson, Lawrie McMenemy, Tony Adams, Mark Lawrenson, David Davies, Bob Harris, Alan

Smith, Rogan Taylor and Gary Owen, all of whom were happy to speak on the record.

Thanks also to all those in and connected to the game who were willing to offer insight and background information but were unwilling to be quoted, for some obvious reasons. They know who they are and naturally I would not embarrass them by naming them.

At the *Mail on Sunday* my Sports Editor, Malcolm Vallerius, has always been a supportive figure, while I have leant on the knowledge, too, of my colleagues Alex Montgomery, Dan King, Joe Bernstein and Peter Higgs.

Heartfelt thanks to my partner Vikki Orvice, who provided loving support and much perceptive editorial input and even interviewed David Ginola for me. My gratitude extends to my son Jack for the times he fed me well when I was writing.

My literary agent, David Luxton of the Luxton-Harris agency, keen fan of words and football, was also a source of inspiration and encouragement, while Rory Scarfe at Simon and Schuster kept me on track.

I am especially thankful for the moral and spiritual support provided by Ian Chapman at Simon and Schuster, long-time corner-man Bruce Lloyd, and a man without whom nothing would be possible these days and who has been a best friend for twenty years now, Bill W.

Ian Ridley,

St Albans, August 2008

1

Coming Home

I can remember when,
I was just a boy of ten,
Hanging around the old Quayside.
'Cause that was when coal was king,
The river was a living thing,
And I was just a boy but it was mine,
The coaly Tyne.

This was a big river,
I want you all to know,
That I was proud.
This was a big river,
I want you all to know,
But that was long ago.
That's not now, That's not now.

'BIG RIVER', JIMMY NAIL

Driving in from the A1 on the A189 over the Redheugh Bridge, the huge elevated road that spans the Tyne and links Gateshead with Newcastle, the view is spectacular. It has grown more so with the passing of the years, the increased prosperity of the region and the consequent ambition of the architecture.

Down to the left is the Metro Radio Arena, where you can be entertained by anything from the Combat Fighting Championship through Def Leppard and Whitesnake to a meeting of angry Northern Rock shareholders. Along the river to the right is the vast new Sage complex, which resembles a giant armadillo and has become a major music venue. Panning back from there, the eye is briefly drawn to St Nicholas's Cathedral, long since dwarfed by another, more modern, hilltop place of worship; a towering, almost vertiginous structure that now dominates the landscape and has become the focal point of this city and community.

This is St James' Park, home of Newcastle United Football Club. And, this midwinter of 2008 as I drive into the city, home once again to Kevin Keegan. He has been called the Messiah to the point of clichéd tedium. Saviour or not, he has certainly been the city's on-off lover for more than twenty-five years as both player and manager; this, in the role of the latter, was his second coming.

All who know the place and club insist that any manager has to 'get' Newcastle; that they must know the warmth of its people and understand the aspirations of the football club's support. They would like to compete with the modern English game's 'Big Four' of Manchester United, Chelsea, Arsenal and Liverpool – all clubs that differ from Newcastle in that they are not the only top-flight club in their respective cities – but they want, too, their football played with a swagger.

Sam Allardyce never quite got it, according to the fans. Prior to being brought in by the club's then chairman, Freddy Shepherd, in the early summer of 2007, he had led Bolton Wanderers into the Premiership and kept them there for six seasons as well as taking them into Europe. Allardyce sought to bring his brand of scientific methodology and functional football to St James' but Tyneside turned on him. Results were averagely acceptable, with the team placed eleventh in the table, but the style was significantly lacking.

In June 2007, shortly after Allardyce's appointment, the club was subject to new ownership with the completion of a takeover by the apparently reclusive Mike Ashley, who came in at Number 25 on Britain's Rich List with a personal fortune of £1.9billion from his Sports Direct leisurewear company. The purchase of the club cost Ashley £134million, with another £100million to settle debts.

Generally speaking, football-club power brokers who inherit managers rarely warm to them and instead look for the earliest opportunity to dismiss them. So it was with Ashley and Allardyce. Ashley had demonstrated his ruthlessness in the summer of 2007 by dismissing Shepherd from the club while he was ill in hospital. The loss went unlamented by the fans, but for Shepherd there was consolation in the £38million he received for his stake in the club.

With Shepherd gone, Allardyce was always vulnerable and by early January 2008 he too was out, just twenty-four games and eight months into a three-year contract. Ashley had been contemplating the sacking since as far back as November.

Ashley's great friend and former business associate Paul Kemsley, formerly vice-chairman of Tottenham Hotspur, recommended Harry Redknapp as Allardyce's replacement. Redknapp's Portsmouth had been playing with the sort of panache that Ashley wanted, had just won 4–1 at St James'. Kemsley sounded him out. During the week of an England international against Croatia, Redknapp travelled to Barbados to relax and think the proposition over. On his return, he declined.

But back came Ashley after Allardyce's side lost three games in a row over Christmas then drew limply 0–0 at Stoke in the FA Cup. Allardyce would later say that he was never given enough time, that it was like being asked to construct the Empire State Building in a month, but few were listening.

The nation endured a few days of will-he/won't-he with Redknapp, a figure who has always given the impression of enjoying the intrigue and gossip of the game. Newcastle believed that this time he would take the job. Redknapp in the end decided that, aged sixty, he was comfortable staying on the South Coast. The offer of a helicopter so that he could remain living at his home on Sandbanks, near Poole, did not appeal; neither did the chance to double his salary of around £1.5million. By now he had built up a good sum from the game, enough to give him choices.

Thus grew the pressure on Ashley to find someone who would rekindle the club's passion and deliver a team of substance. He did what most owners do in such circumstances. He went for the populist, popular choice, the great black-and-white hope. Out from the hat popped the rabbit: Comeback Kevin.

Keegan would, at the very least, certainly get Newcastle. Growing up in a mining family in 1950s Doncaster, where his family had moved from the North-East in search of work, Keegan was brought up hearing tales of the mighty Magpies and their hero Jackie Milburn at his father Joe's knee. Keegan understood Newcastle like Sir Bobby Robson did before him.

'Well, it's a one-team city and that's crucial,' says Sir Bobby when you ask him to analyse the place. Newcastle manager from 1999 to 2004, he grew up in Langley Park, County

Durham, where half the village was black-and-white and the other half the red-and-white of Sunderland. His eyes mist at the memories as he draws from the depth of feeling for city, club and its favoured sons.

'My dad was Newcastle through and through. He was a coalminer and went to work white and came home black. Loved United. Took me as a boy. I remember Frank Brennan, Bobby Mitchell, Jackie Milburn, the two Robledo brothers, little Ernie Taylor – midget inside-forward, clever player – Powell and Corbett, the two full-backs.

'The catchment area around the city is something like 700,000, maybe up to 1.25million because people can come from a sixty-mile radius. The people are very vibrant, very enthusiastic, knowledgeable and extremely faithful. They are warm, courteous to the players, a bit rugged, friendly and welcoming. Just a very special breed.

'They love the club and just want something to happen all the time. There is a fervour there,' adds the man who also managed Barcelona and England. 'You couldn't walk in the town without being recognised. I had that in Barça. Player or manager, you're spotted and identified straight away, besieged with requests for autographs.

'They are Catalans who don't consider themselves Spanish. So Newcastle have the Geordies who are a race apart and speak a broad tongue. If a real Geordie is in full flow, you wouldn't understand him. I'm talking about Paul Gascoigne. Chris Waddle, Peter Beardsley and Bryan Robson would try to be more polite and speak English. With Gazza, my assistant Don Howe used to ask, "What did he say?" Gascoigne would do it on purpose sometimes. He was a real Geordie lad.

'The loyalty of the support is quite amazing, with what they haven't achieved,' Robson goes on, underplaying his own success: he twice took Newcastle to the Champions League with finishes of third and fourth, which seems remarkable these days given the self-perpetuating dominance of those Big Four clubs. He is well aware, however, that it is more than half a century since the club's last domestic trophy, the FA Cup, and more than eighty since they were champions of England – though they did win the Inter Cities Fairs Cup, the precursor to the UEFA Cup, in 1969.

'They are an expecting public but any owner is lucky that 52,000 will still go every Saturday, hail, rain, shine or blow. They will never shun the club,' he adds. And Keegan's place in all this? 'He became a much-loved son and had a great rapport with everybody.'

Keegan first came to Newcastle towards the end of a most glittering playing career with Liverpool, Hamburg and Southampton that saw him twice crowned European Footballer of the Year and play sixty-three times for England. He had captained his country and was a bubble-permed trendsetter who in the seventies became the nation's superstar. By 1982, at the age of thirty-one, he wanted a swansong at the club whose legend had filled his childhood.

Keegan galvanised the Geordies, leading them into the top flight before departing, after two seasons, to retirement in Spain via a helicopter. He returned eight years later to manage them with an ultimately flawed but nonetheless energising *élan* for five years during one of the golden periods for the English game. From the early to mid-nineties Newcastle entertained royally with the likes of David Ginola, Les Ferdinand and Tino Asprilla but in 1996 famously, sadly, blew a twelve-point lead at the top of the Premiership, their season encapsulated in a 4–3 defeat at Liverpool in what probably remains the finest English club game of the modern era.

Keegan left the club in 1997. Following a sad spell as England manager and a patchy tenure at Manchester City, he had been in Glasgow setting up a pet project called Soccer Circus – a sort of cross between football coaching and theme park, designed mainly to get kids interested, through entertainment, in the game. Now, as an antidote to Allardyce, the great romantic was back from exile.

The question was whether such romanticism could survive and thrive again in the pragmatic Premier League, whether a storm-tossed support would this time give him time and adulation. Life, the game, had moved on. Even Arsenal, delivering the closest thing to the type of fluent football to which Keegan aspired, were the product of a clinical mind with an attention to detail, in their multilayered coach Arsene Wenger, rather than the broad-brush approach favoured by Keegan. And Keegan was out of touch, having by his own admission watched little football of late. The city, too, had changed.

I am from Northumberland stock myself, with a North-East surname, and was also as a boy informed of the club's folklore. In the early morning of Saturday 23 February during the 2007–08 season, I drove over Redheugh Bridge. Newcastle's match against the current champions, Manchester United, would not kick off until teatime; the city was still stirring itself for the weekend. It offered a window, in time and opportunity, to see what Keegan was walking back into.

The great thing about Newcastle is that it is a city you can walk around. Perhaps this is why – strangely, to someone living in the South and for a place so big – you can usually find a vacant parking meter easily enough. The railway station is at its heart, St James' a short stroll away, which is delightful in these days of stadiums often being inaccessible except by car. In fact, everything in Newcastle is a short stroll away, its central attractions revealing one foot in the past culture of coalmining and shipbuilding and the other in the modern service industries.

Turn right out of the station and head for the Quayside down Westgate Street and you will pass the remarkable oasis of the Grade II-listed Literary and Philosophical Society building, England's largest independent library outside London, with more than 150,000 books and 16,000 music recordings.

Its quiet is in marked contrast as you press on past bars like the Viper Lounge and Jimmyz, the names more redolent of young movie-star brats overdosing in Los Angeles or Formula One drivers quaffing Champagne in Monte Carlo. Once at the river, you reach the Malmaison Hotel on the site of the old Co-Op building, a fleet of silver Mercedes on call outside.

From here are revealed the Tyne bridges in all their glory. After the Redheugh comes the superb King Edward VII Rail Bridge with its semicircular construction, then the Queen Elizabeth II Metro Bridge, the High Level Bridge, the Swing Bridge and the Tyne Bridge. To which collection has been added the Gateshead Millennium Footbridge, which looks something like that in London linking St Paul's to the Tate Modern, and also resembles the Wembley arch. It's known locally as the Blinking Eye for the way it opens to allow shipping to pass.

Evident here, too, is the juxtaposition of old and new, the meeting of past poverty and contemporary prosperity. On the banks of the river, the sooty granite of the old terraced buildings contrasts with the glass of the shops and offices. By the medieval wall, near the rebuilt structure of the new castle from which the city's name derives, is a sign for Bessie Surtees' house, family home of the wife of John Scott, Lord Chancellor of England in the late 1700s. Further into town is the obelisk monument to Earl Grey, Northumberland son and Prime Minister from 1830 to 1834, who also gave his name to a perfumed tea not quite as popular after four p.m. round here as it is in the salons down South.

Sir Bobby Robson's words reflect pride in that old and new. 'It's a great city and it's changed,' he says. 'The Quayside, the Metro Centre, the airport, the A1 link, the train service to London every half-hour. And the airport: you can fly to Dubai, Amsterdam, Paris, Prague, Rome, you know. Direct from Newcastle.'

The river might once have heaved with traffic but now only an old ferry, the *Tuxedo Princess* out of Stranraer, sits moored, a beer advert on its side hinting at its modern function as a nightclub.

On that Saturday in February I crossed the footbridge to Gateshead, wobbling as I went, and arrived at the old Baltic flour mill, which is now a centre for modern art. Nearby, up on the hill, is the striking Sage, before you reach the huge Hilton Hotel.

Earlier in the week it had emerged that Paul Gascoigne, another of Newcastle's favourite sons, had fallen on times harder than even he had known before. He's actually from this Gateshead side of the city, and had just lately been living in the Malmaison and Hilton hotels.

The kid described as 'daft as a brush' by Sir Bob is actually now a fully grown alcoholic and addict, who on top of everything else may be suffering from Attention Deficit Hyperactivity Disorder. Certainly he appears to share many characteristics with those diagnosed with the illness: gifted, physically agile, seemingly confident and successful but lacking in self-esteem at heart and being full of nervous energy and prone to self-sabotage. Gazza has three times been through rehab and three times relapsed frighteningly.

In his loneliness, and craving the phoney companionship that hotels can provide, he went stir-crazy and was sectioned in a psychiatric unit. Looking at this modern Lubyanka that is the towering Hilton, you get a sense of his pain. Nearby are the old high-rises and terraces of Dunston where he grew up. Like most modern cities, Newcastle's central opulence is surrounded by reminders of neighbouring paucity and poverty. A shop on Mosley Street called The Mint is a case in point. 'We cash cheques,' declares a sign outside. 'Pay-day advances up to £400.'

I passed a gaggle of young women walking from the station, pulling wheeled suitcases, their giggles sounding their intent – a warning of what to expect later in one of the country's top hen- and stag-night venues. All sported pink fluorescent wigs; one or two wore the sort of plastic breasts with which Gazza, then regarded as madcap as opposed to ill, regaled the nation on his tear-stained return from the 1990 World Cup.

To the match, and up through Chinatown where an ornate statue proclaiming the district sits alongside the Tyneside Irish Centre. Just down the road is a sports bookshop, The Back Page. It boasts a whole wall of Newcastle literature, from the angst-ridden assessments of *Newcastle United: Fifty Years of Hurt* to the satirical *And You Wonder Why We Drink: Newcastle United and the Quest for the Intertoto Cup*. There's a book about the club's famous Number 9 strikers down the years, *Shirt of Legends*. *Short of Legends* might be more apt.

For at this point, in February, Newcastle were struggling. Keegan's return, just under six weeks previously, was greeted with the wildly optimistic scenes he has often provoked in these parts but had yet to have the desired effect. The night he was appointed, a few days after a crushing and embarrassing 6–0 defeat at Manchester United that followed the 0–0 draw at Stoke, Newcastle did manage to beat the Championship side (who went on to be promoted) by 4–1 in the replay; but it was the prelude to things getting worse rather than better.

The next four League games yielded just two points and two goals, with eight conceded – and a 3–0 FA Cup defeat by Arsenal simply adding to the woes. Only Reading, who would go on to be relegated, were faring worse in the Premier League's form table. With Manchester United the visitors again to St James', it was not looking good. The days when United came here and lost 5–0 during Keegan's first managerial incarnation were just over eleven years past but felt like aeons ago.

In the local *Evening Chronicle*, under a back-page headline of 'Sweat Blood for United', Keegan was calling for maximum effort from his players, urging them to get in an early tackle or to bravely put in head or foot to lift the crowd and get them behind the team in the way he recalled them doing in the eighties. It was Keegan at his drum-banging best, though the subtext was clear: here was a realist whose team were far behind Manchester United, a side beginning to crank up the pressure on Arsenal at the top of the table.

There was a curious mood among the support walking to the game; anticipation of a big match for sure but a sense of pragmatic awareness also. The Mags were not playing well – were a bit of a mess, in fact – and taking a point from the game would represent a major triumph.

In the press room, gallows humour abounded among the local reporters. This was in contrast to the upbeat nature of their coverage, something that their sports editors probably demanded early in Keegan's latest reign. They had, after all, endured plenty this season – for many seasons, really. The atmosphere recalled a line in the baseball movie *Bull Durham* where the announcer declares: 'I have seen enough to know that I have seen too much.'

Outside, home fans gathered to await the arrival of the team buses. Suddenly there were loud jeers.

'That'll be Man United,' I ventured to a local journalist.

'More probably Newcastle,' he replied.

Newcastle and Keegan did get a good reception, however, as they usually do if the fans feel some hope of light at the end of the tunnel. With 52,291 crowded inside the stadium it seemed that their appetite was astonishingly undiminished, had even grown, since Keegan's previous spell here.

'When I was there they were just putting the finishing

touches to the upper-deck steel structure to take the capacity up from 37,000 to 52,000,' says Sir Bobby. 'If you sit on the seventh floor you can actually see the sea at Tynemouth, twelve miles away. The players are tiny. You won't see their faces, you won't see their numbers, but still they sell out.'

One disappointment was that 'Coming Home', Mark Knopfler's haunting guitar music from the film *Local Hero*, was no longer the tune to which Newcastle ran out, as it had been during Keegan's last tenure at St James'. It had perfectly mirrored the stirring Keegan era and was guaranteed to get the hairs on the back of the neck standing, its heartwarming strains evoking the spirit of the city and its football. Instead we now had a feeble rendition of *The Blaydon Races* (written by one George Ridley) that somehow diluted the atmosphere as opposed to enhancing it. Only when a chorus of Geordie voices sang the song did it have an impact; this single-voice version had none.

Initially it looked as though Keegan had persuaded his players to forget the results of the previous month, as Michael Owen went close with the game's first chance. It was, however, a false dawn – a phrase that could have been coined for the club. Soon the absence of confidence in the Newcastle side became clear; soon United were pouring through gaping holes in the home side caused by apprehension and, worse, lack of legs and effort. The likes of Nicky Butt, Alan Smith and Damien Duff, all off the pace, were being played through and round by a younger, more vibrant United whose football was as quick and slick as Keegan's sides used to be. This one he had inherited was ponderous by contrast.

Midway through the first half Man United took the lead, when Wayne Rooney turned home Cristiano Ronaldo's cross and Newcastle were caught by the old one-two performed by two new, sensational talents. Now United's travelling support began to taunt the home manager, who was trying to look unperturbed on the touchline. 'Keegan is back,' they sang mockingly, adding for bad measure: 'Keegan for England.'

When Ronaldo doubled United's lead just before half-time, Keegan could not prevent a look of disgust with his team appearing on his face. His was a face that had turned fifty-seven on Valentine's Day, just nine days earlier, and that had aged considerably since we had seen him depart Manchester City. Around its more deeply etched lines the hair was now silver as opposed to grey. The change had taken some of us by surprise. Though we too had aged, you never quite see it in yourself as you do in someone else.

It prompted worried words from another former England manager bitten by the job and the game. As Graham Taylor wrote in a forthright column in the *Daily Telegraph*, Keegan now appeared weary whenever he spoke on television.

'What concerns me is when I see Keegan being interviewed,' Taylor noted. 'Like almost everyone else, prior to his departure from Manchester City three seasons ago, I was used to seeing the sparkle and glint in his eyes – which to me represents fire in your belly – but now I am witnessing a tired look, eyes that keep moving about, not looking directly at the person who posed the question. Is it because he does not know the answers?'

Had Keegan just got them into half-time only a goal behind they might yet have had a chance . . . Now, at two down, the chances were slim, especially with the difference in performance and condition of the two teams, one of whom were short on belief, the other brimming with it.

The PA announcer knew as much. The interval raffle was drawn and a bottle of whisky presented.

'You might need it,' he said as the holder of the lucky number grabbed it hastily.

Sensitively and touchingly, given the week's news about Gazza, the DJ played the Pink Floyd epic 'Shine On You Crazy Diamond'. This was a city that not only loved its own but also felt for its own. As Sir Bobby had told me: 'They never forget you. It's a great city to play football in, I'll tell you.'

In the sanctuary of the dressing-room, meanwhile, in what coaches call the golden ten minutes, Keegan was using half-time to convey to his team that the next goal could well be decisive.

'I could only be honest with them,' he would say later in that open way of his. 'We all knew that the next goal would be crucial.' Get it back to 2–1 and United might wobble. The unspoken part was that to go 3–0 down would mean the end.

Newcastle did get an early chance in the second half, as they had done in the first, but Edwin Van Der Sar in the visitors' goal kept out a shot with his knee from the otherwise indolent Duff. Newcastle needed a goal but it was United who got it. Soon Ronaldo grabbed his own second and his side's third as a result of another swift movement far too incisive for Newcastle.

Abdoulaye Faye, the Senegal international and one of the few impressive signings that Allardyce made with £26million advanced, did pull a goal back but it was a token gesture. Rooney curled home exquisitely from the edge of the area for his second and the substitute Louis Saha sealed a five-goal romp, some revenge for the United manager Sir Alex Ferguson for that result of more than a decade ago against Keegan, even if he and his United had enjoyed life much more since.

At the final whistle, Ferguson did his best but there was no avoiding it. Keegan strode over to embrace him, to pat him on the back of the head with one hand and on a cheek with the other in his trademark end-of-match move. It's a less threatening version of the 'happy slapping' popular with kids, but it's scarcely less dangerous and to be endured rather than enjoyed by rival managers.

It was a crushing result for Newcastle but no one was ready yet to turn on Keegan. The crowd realised that he would take some time to shed Allardyce's skin and it was an overpaid, underachieving bunch of players who were most to blame. Keegan probably knew as much as well but also realised that he would get nothing out of them if he emphasised it in

public. For now, he patted every one of them on the back as they left the field. He had always been that type of players' man.

However, the situation for Newcastle was getting serious now. They were in thirteenth position, stuck on twenty-eight points, just six above the relegation places. While it may not yet have seemed especially desperate, it was getting difficult to see where the next points were coming from and Keegan knew it. The Messiah? He was in danger of becoming the man who put the 'mess' into that word.

'We need to win a football match for the players,' he said when he arrived at his press conference. 'We need forty points and everybody who has not got forty points can go down. West Ham did once. We need four wins.' This statement was perhaps unduly pessimistic in this season, where a club was likely to stay up with several points fewer than that, but he was obviously setting a target so that his players would not think their task easier than it was.

Keegan has always had a reputation for openness, has always insisted that it's what the Geordie fans appreciate. A famous example of this trait in action occurred during his previous spell at St James', when he bravely stood on the club steps to explain to an angry gathering of supporters why he was selling top scorer Andy Cole to Manchester United.

'I think this is an honest and caring group of players and I wouldn't say that if I didn't believe it,' he now said. 'But sometimes honest and caring is not enough in the Premier

League. You need to be a bit clever and streetwise. And you certainly need to show better concentration than we had in certain situations tonight. The players' effort was good but once the concentration went the confidence did too.'

There was a word for that remarkable crowd, too. 'We have lost 5–1 at home and they have stuck with us all the way,' he said. He knew them so well. He also knew that it was embarrassing that the reward for all the revenue they generated was little but a soap opera. And that in front of a live, national television audience.

All this was useful stuff for us journalists, all very quotable for the next day's paper. And with Saturday night now being eaten into, and edition times coming and going, all were anxious to get their work done and be on their way.

There was, however, that object of modern parlance among us: the elephant in the room; that which people needed to pluck up courage to ask. For we understood that Keegan could become prickly, these days more than ever before as experience with the media, particularly the written press, had soured him. After all, his honesty had sometimes been used against him while those in the game less forthcoming and communicative received less criticism.

The concern with Keegan has always been that he would get going when the going got tough. It is well remembered that during his first spell at Newcastle he threatened to walk out after just a month in charge. He had felt that he was not getting the financial backing he'd been promised. 'It's not like the brochure,' he said in his usual catchy manner. It wasn't long before St James' then purse-holder, Sir John Hall, was persuading him to stay.

Before he finally did quit there were other occasions when he had threatened to do so. He had walked from England, from Manchester City, too, at unexpected moments when he felt overwhelmed by circumstances. Might he do it again here and now after a draining and demoralising first month?

It was time to widen the discussion. Did he wonder, I asked him, whether he needed all this grief and aggravation any more, what with some of the chants he was getting from opposition fans, what with the results that were coming?

'What do you mean?' he asked. He sought to look baffled but I sensed that he knew exactly what I meant. I repeated the question. He grew agitated.

'I am here for three and half years,' he said. 'That's what I have signed for.'

There was a pause and a silence before he went on. Most people in the room were uncomfortable but were keen to hear his response. Often in such situations, if you bear the silence rather than embarrassedly change the subject, the interviewee will break the silence and elaborate quotably.

'This is a club I love and this is a club I want to take back where it belongs,' he said at last. 'My commitment is 110 per cent and you can't give any more than that.

'I took the job with sixteen games to go and I knew there were some tough games to come – Arsenal away twice, Aston

Villa, Manchester United . . . I was well aware of the challenge but I am still optimistic.'

This was pure and vintage Keegan, and highlighted a variety of idiosyncrasies. He was wounded by the implication that he might be a quitter; this had touched a nerve. Then he grew defiant in defence of his position. Finally there was that relentlessly positive outlook that had somehow survived all the knocks he has taken down the years. At this juncture his optimism stood rekindled by the new challenge he'd been presented but it would be severely tested in the months ahead.

We had our story – '"I Won't Quit", Keegan Vows' in answer to the readers asking the same question themselves – and Keegan departed, leaving us to write it.

By now St James' was deserted, having seemingly decamped *en masse* to the city centre just a few hundred yards away. The football day may have been done but, despite another bad result, it wouldn't be long before a night of revelry was in full swing.

For some it already was. On the walk back through the legendary Bigg Market, where bar after bar was patrolled by bouncers, young men and women were in uniform. Jeans and short-sleeved shirts outside the trousers for one, short dresses revealing white goose-pimpled thighs for the other. I was definitely getting old. I feared these poor young things would catch their deaths of cold. I worried that the blonde falling about in the gutter was going to burn herself on the cigarette she was determinedly clinging on to.

'It's mad. I never went there once. I couldn't. I would get mobbed. You stay away,' Sir Bobby Robson told me, echoing what most players of his day soon made of the harassment – largely benign but with the potential to turn and make the papers – that accompanied any visit. 'They tell me it's sensational, mind,' he added.

Sir Bobby and his contemporaries differ in this respect from the current team and its owners. Soon Mike Ashley and his mates would be down here to drink in Tiger, Tiger or some such watering hole, enjoying the popularity and profile they had bought – though it may have been somewhat diluted on this particular night.

Keegan, meanwhile, would be contemplating yet another defeat, wondering what the near future held. He may have talked about being in it for the long haul, but the doubts would return. Besides, was the owner here for the long term? Would Keegan be given the choice to stay?

The desire may have been to re-create a glorious era but much had changed in terms of circumstance, city and people. This was indeed a big river but that was long ago, as Jimmy Nail had sung.

Playing for and then managing Newcastle United may well have been roles that Kevin Keegan was born to perform, but three strikes at it . . .?

2

The Kid

The young look at older figures sometimes, when those twin thieves of time and age have wrought their mischief, and struggle to reconcile reports both verbal and written, the pictures from the past and the action replays, with what they now see before them. So it is with the silver-haired Kevin Keegan. Was he really that potent, that vibrant, that good as a player? Was he really that famous?

The answer to all of the above is yes.

Once he arrived at the top level of English football, with Liverpool then the undisputed dominant force, Keegan proceeded to become the domestic game's biggest star of the seventies and early eighties. On the field he became Bill Shankly's talisman, the idol of Anfield, as Liverpool accumulated League titles and a European Cup. In a move that shocked everyone he then took off to West Germany for a spell with Hamburg before creating even more waves by returning to play for sleepy Southampton, the prelude to his playing finale at Newcastle United.

Through it all, he was the lynchpin of the England team,

playing first under Sir Alf Ramsey then becoming a central figure in the teams of Don Revie, Joe Mercer and Ron Greenwood, who made him captain, before an acrimonious dumping by Bobby Robson.

Keegan's emergence on the football field came in an altogether less colourful age, socially speaking – after the so-called swinging sixties, when postwar austerity had finally given way to a more liberal mood and culture. In the seventies recession and strikes bit under Labour prime ministers Harold Wilson and James Callaghan before the 'Winter of Discontent' of 1978/79 all but forced Callaghan into calling a General Election, which saw Margaret Thatcher elected in 1979.

In the sixties George Best had been the handsome, dashing symbol of the game. On the field his long hair flowed as his bravery and ball skills carried him past defenders; off the field his charisma brought him celebrity and riches beyond the realms of football as he became Britain's first modern superstar for the television age, moving comfortably into the worlds of fashion and showbusiness.

Best and his club, Manchester United, were unprepared for the attention that came his way, however, and it almost ate him alive. Through it all, his alcoholism worsened. Best would have been alcoholic anyway – it was his destiny and personality – but his madcap existence accentuated his fears and anxieties and accelerated an illness about which little was then known, and from which he could not recover. Indeed, he later stubbornly refused to recover from his illness and it killed him prematurely.

Keegan by his own admission was never the natural talent that was Best. Rather he described himself with self-deprecation and accuracy as 'the mongrel who made it to Crufts'. Keegan was, though, dependable and without waywardness and therefore became attractive to advertisers and marketing men.

Unknowingly and unwittingly Keegan profited from the George Best experience. Post-Best, there were agents and accountants more aware of both the pitfalls and the potential, of the commercial possibilities of the game in a burgeoning media era. Keegan grew to be famous, feted and financially secure, the last-named as a result not just of football's increasing wages (still way short of today's sums) but also of all the external opportunities his position brought about.

The bedevilled Paul Gascoigne was English football's most minutely observed object of anxiety of the nineties, as scrutinised as was Princess Diana in the 'real' life of the era. If Gazza was the heir to Best's hedonistic title, then the shooting star of the new millennium, the reliable and upright David Beckham, was the natural successor to Keegan. Beckham made much of his Number 7 shirt at Manchester United and as captain of England. Keegan was the original, even wore the number on a gold chain around his neck.

'Imagine him today,' says Bob Harris, *News of the World* sportswriter who ghosted Keegan's autobiography. 'He was big enough at that time when football was back page and not front – thank God – but today he would be massive. He was at the vanguard of superstars, the hair, the adverts, the television.'

That permed hair, the vogue of the day that many who copied it look back on with a mixture of nostalgia and horror, certainly projected Keegan. There were the iconic Brut TV ads in which, along with Britain's best-loved boxer, Henry Cooper, he plugged a cheap cologne just as cosmetics for men were becoming acceptable, urging us to 'splash it all over'.

He was also a face of the government's Green Cross Code road-safety campaign: gold chain, check jacket, flared trousers rampant and showing a kid how to cross Anfield Road outside the Kop end. 'Be smart, be safe,' he exhorted.

Rogan Taylor, founder of the Football Supporters' Association, senior lecturer at Liverpool University's management school and perceptive sociologist when it comes to the game, recognises Keegan's place in the scheme of things.

'He was the first British footballer to take hold of the concept of the personal brand,' he says. 'And he managed his way through the jungle that swallowed George Best. He knew also how to leverage that brand, a phrase that is commonplace now but in those days nobody would have understood. He was way ahead of his time.'

Keegan also appeared on a TV show called *Superstars*, which drew huge ratings in the days before the current myriad channels, a multi-discipline sporting challenge and one of those touchstone programmes of the seventies. The vision of him painfully falling off a bicycle round a cinder athletics track became the talk of the nation in office, factory and playground – what would now be called a watercooler moment. He sang in public, appeared on *This Is Your Life*. The boy who was taken by his dad to the pictures in Doncaster to see Deborah Kerr in *The King and I* would get to meet her in Spain. And he kissed Margaret Thatcher on the cheek for a photoshoot.

That in particular said much about the pragmatic Keegan, who came from pure working-class stock. We all are clearly shaped by our backgrounds but he was never shackled by his.

'A lot of people form their characters in stages. Kevin was formed very early on and developed from there,' says Bob Harris, having chronicled the subject in depth. 'You move into different sections of society as footballers do and your persona changes, your style of life, but Kevin remained Kevin.'

What would Keegan's father have made of such intimacy with a Tory prime minister? Dad Joe, a miner and staunch Labour voter, once turned down a local Conservative Association's request to use the family's house as a canvassing centre, even though it would have brought in a good sum of money. But Kevin, who had developed a keen eye for a financial deal, had long since left behind his roots, outgrown his humble background. A fascinating background it was, too; almost the archetypal upbringing of a working-class hero.

Kevin Keegan was born in the mining village of Armthorpe near Doncaster on 14 February 1951 to an Irish Catholic family who had first settled in Stanley, near Newcastle, where his grandfather Frank could find work in the Burns coalfield. Keegan later took great pride when he discovered after moving to Tyneside that his granddad had been one of the heroes of a pit disaster in 1909 at the West Stanley mine, helping to rescue some thirty men.

Work was again the purpose of the family's move further south, with Frank's son Joe also becoming a miner, at Markham Main colliery. It was Joe who first made Kevin aware of Newcastle United, regaling him with tales of his own childhood watching Jackie Milburn and Hughie Gallagher. One of Keegan's regrets was that his father died, aged seventy-one, in 1976 and did not get to see him play for Newcastle.

Kevin is actually Keegan's middle name. In accordance with family tradition he was given his father's name, Joseph, but Kevin stuck. There must have been some kind of premonition that he would be no ordinary Joe.

Keegan's childhood was meagre – almost Spartan – but evidently content, based on the binding ties of the more enveloping community spirit of the fifties that was particularly apparent in mining areas. The family, comprising dad

Joe, mum Doris, sister Mary and Keegan's younger brother, Michael, moved from Armthorpe into a terraced house in Doncaster itself, with a zinc bath in an outhouse and a toilet at the bottom of the garden. The house was lit by gas and the biggest room was a cellar for the coal.

Working on the Jesuit principle that the boy by seven years old is indicative of the man he will become, when we examine Keegan's past certain experiences seem to be clearly formative in that they led him to develop some of the characteristic traits he displayed in later life. In this way it's possible to see the beginnings of his gravitation towards greater prosperity and his desire to get for himself some of the wealth he saw.

Keegan developed a friendship with a lad called Maurice Freedman, whose father worked on the railways and was well off enough to afford electricity and a television in the house – rare in those days. It was in Freedman's house that Keegan first saw flickering images of professional football, watching Wolverhampton Wanderers, then the country's biggest team, capturing the nation's imagination by playing the first floodlit games, against the likes of Honved of Hungary. Billy Wright, the Wolves and England captain, became a Keegan favourite as he was not the conventional tall centre-half and Keegan was growing aware that he was a small lad too.

Together Freedman and Keegan also made good use of living near what was a big centre for horseracing. They set themselves up at a local stables to wash the cars of the men attending the racehorse sales and, by cleverly going where the money was, they made good profits. Keegan also got his first taste of publicity: when the stables closed, the local paper, Doncaster's *Evening Post*, pictured the two lads looking glum and sitting on their buckets.

'He came from a poor family and working-class area and he was always very aware of that,' says Harris. 'Hence the going out and cleaning cars. He might get a wedge off a guy who's done well with the horses. There was nothing wrong with his brain at all. He was a very bright guy and a worker, never afraid to get his hands dirty. Rolling up his sleeves was never a problem for him.'

In later life Keegan became passionate about horses and racing and this interest clearly stems from their central role in Doncaster. The racecourse was the home of the St Leger and the meeting offered a chance for the town to don its finery. It was at the fair connected to the event that Keegan in his late teens met Jean, who would become his wife.

A win on the horses for his father also furnished Keegan with his first pair of football boots. He used them not to strike goals in one penalty area, though, but to stop them in the other. Keegan, as was common among children growing up in mining communities, suffered from croup and was unable to run too much in the outfield; thus he became a goalkeeper.

By age nine he had a curious choice of footballing hero, too. Keegan had watched and, like everyone else who saw it and later revered it – notably Sir Alex Ferguson – been enthralled by the 1960 European Cup Final, in which Real Madrid beat Eintracht Frankfurt 7–3 in front of more than 127,000 people at Glasgow's Hampden Park. Not for him Ferenc Puskas or Alfredo di Stefano. Keegan took to wearing a flat cap in goal because he liked how the hapless German goalkeeper Egon Loy looked in one. Keegan would also stand behind the goal at Doncaster Rovers' Belle Vue ground observing his goalkeeping hero Willie Nimmo, who would later be one of the guests on Keegan's *This Is Your Life*.

It was while attending St Francis Xavier school, however, that Keegan encountered his first serious footballing influence: a nun named Sister Mary Oliver, who took the school football lessons in the absence of another teacher. She refereed matches in full habit, crucifix swinging. 'We could never argue with decisions,' Keegan would say, 'because they were coming from the very top.'

It was Sister Mary who encouraged Keegan; when he eventually reached the top of the game all the papers wanted pictures of the two of them together. He would say that it was because of her that he saw that football grounds were like churches: they're all very well as buildings but it takes people to bring them alive.

Through his teenage years Keegan grew worried – and that was about the sum of it. While his peers sprouted up, his height remained five feet for several years. At secondary school, St Peter's in Cantley, the goals were higher and he had to give up the goalkeeping to play outfield. There was no immediate success. He failed to make the Doncaster Boys team and, while he was not actually rejected by the parent club, since he turned up at the wrong place for a trial, he was certainly missed. This was largely because in his early teens Keegan was easily overlooked, both literally and metaphorically.

Years later the big Geordie ex-Guardsman Lawrie McMenemy would manage Doncaster Rovers before going to Southampton, where he pulled off the coup of signing Keegan.

'It used to crop up a lot at Doncaster, that Kevin Keegan was turned down by the club,' says McMenemy now. 'I used to say, "Well, I wasn't here then."' McMenemy likens Keegan to another player he had at Southampton – a 1966 World Cup winner, no less.

'Kevin was like Alan Ball. They had so much in common. If you look at their careers, both were knocked back by their local clubs because of their size and both said, "I'll show you." And both went on to great things.'

It still took Keegan a while to show anyone. His Uncle Frank, who lived in Nuneaton, fixed him up with a summer trial for Coventry City, a team then managed by Jimmy Hill. Keegan made it to the final two but was eventually released. He was hurt by the rejection but encouraged that he had made it so far.

Perhaps it was Keegan's size that made him a joker at school, in the way that little men sometimes feel the need to get themselves noticed. Whatever the reason for it, his comedic tendency did not always make him popular with teaching staff. School reports are often perceptive and have an amusing relevance in later life, even when they're wide of the mark. One of Keegan's noted that: 'He is an exhibitionist and will do much better when he loses this trait.'

It was surely his size and the rejection he encountered because of it that spurred Keegan's determination to become a footballer. He was certainly imbued with the work ethic that eventually made him what he was. And with determination, too, if not bloody-minded stubbornness. At the age of fifteen he embarked on what now seems like a project fraught with danger: a run from Manchester to Doncaster across the Pennines, with a group of friends in aid of a local orphans' charity. While he could go on no more at the edge of Barnsley, he was the last boy standing.

A career in football seemed like a far-fetched notion when he left school, with two O levels – in art and history – and took up a job as a tea boy and messenger at the Peglers Brass Works in Doncaster. He was soon recruited to the works team's reserves, which necessitated him playing twice on Saturdays: in the morning for the company and in the afternoon for his youth club. On Sundays he played for the Lonsdale House pub team.

Back then there were not the academy systems and copious scouting networks that exist nowadays. Had such things been in place Keegan would have undoubtedly been recruited by some club, no matter how humble, in the Yorkshire region, simply because he had glimpses of real potential – and no club wants to miss out on potential. He would have been given an opportunity to impress in training and drills, and in the odd game here and there. He would certainly not have been allowed to play three times a weekend, but in Keegan's era there was nothing to stop kids playing as much as they chose to.

Keegan needed a lucky break – and got it. Or, rather, he got the sort of break that seems to come to those with some ability, but from which only those with intense determination profit.

One day Keegan, now a right-winger but still not even five-and-a-half feet tall, was playing against Woodfield, a team which included a Bob Nellis. Nellis would go on to chair Doncaster's Rugby League club but at the time was a local youth coach with contacts at Scunthorpe United, by whom he'd been asked to keep an eye open for young talent. During this match he was deputed to mark Keegan, was given the run-around and was impressed enough to make a recommendation.

Nellis drove Keegan over to Scunthorpe for a few trial matches. After playing a game with the first-team squad in the club car park, sometimes used for training, the diminutive but determined kid was offered an apprenticeship at £4 10s a week by Scunthorpe's then manager, Ron Ashman.

Though the wage was less than Keegan had been getting at Peglers, he bit Ashman's hand off.

'What did I need money for? I didn't drink or smoke. I was happy as Larry,' Keegan later said. He was on his way, but a tortuous route it initially proved to be. Without Nellis to drive him the twenty-five miles to Scunthorpe every day, he had to take two buses before hitching a lift the last fifteen miles of the journey. This meant rising at six a.m. for a nine o'clock start.

His situation eased when he reached the age of seventeen. His wages went up to £7 a week – much better, though he would still have to take a job the next summer in a steel works – and the club provided him with digs in Scunthorpe. He took over a room that had become available when the club's goalkeeper, one Ray Clemence, signed for Liverpool. The portents had begun to mount.

'If you look right from Doncaster, you get Scunthorpe,' Lawrie McMenemy notes. 'If you look left, you get Leeds. I often wonder what would have happened to Kevin if he had looked left. He might not have made it into the first team so soon and things might have been different.'

Keegan spent a period in the juniors and reserves in the old Midland League, playing against such then decent non-League teams as Matlock and Grantham, where he learnt how to avoid gnarled old defenders determined to put kids in their place (usually over the pitch-side railings). He then made his Football League debut in 1968, aged just seventeen, against Peterborough United. However, and unlike, for example,

Jimmy Greaves, who scored on every club debut he played, Keegan showed no flourish of introduction. He did not shine and Scunthorpe were beaten.

Nonetheless within a few weeks he found himself in the side to play Arsenal in a League Cup tie at the Old Show Ground in front of a splendid gate of more than 17,000 people. Despite Scunny's 6–1 loss, Keegan impressed Arsenal enough to be invited to go on trial with their youth team to a tournament in Africa. To his sadness, FA rules prevented it and Arsenal, then building under Bertie Mee towards the Double of 1971, did not follow up their interest.

By now Keegan was definitely attracting attention, as teenagers making waves in the lower divisions still do. Bobby Robson, then manager of top-division Ipswich Town, was among those who took a look at him.

'I came away thinking, "Well, a bit small, may not handle the top flight. No better than what I have got,"' he recalls. In hindsight, does he regret letting Keegan slip through? He laughs. 'I should have bought him, yes. I made a mistake but then I only saw him once.'

These days big clubs pay fortunes for the raw material that they believe they can hone by bringing them through their youth team, training with the first team and generally exposing them to the ambience and philosophy of the club so that they are groomed and ready. Arsenal signed Theo Walcott from Southampton aged sixteen, a purchase made on the basis of only his pace and potential. It cost £6million down, rising to £12million should he make a certain number of appearances and win trophies.

Back in the late sixties, however, the prevailing belief was that players were best learning their trade in the lower leagues until they became closer to the finished article and perhaps of more immediate use to the first team. Robson's concerns about Keegan's size – still a little short of the five feet seven he would eventually attain – and consequently about how he might cope physically at the highest levels, seemed to be widespread, too.

This attitude must have rankled, yet Keegan managed to make light of his height. In fact, being the joker that had been identified at school, Keegan would sometimes employ his short stature to entertain the team on the bus, acting as a ventriloquist's dummy while sitting on the knee of Tom Taylor – football reporter for Scunthorpe's *Evening Telegraph* and father of Graham Taylor.

Keegan was constantly being tracked by the bigger clubs, something mentioned in an early BBC television interview conducted by Gerald Sinstadt – one of almost 300 clips of Keegan on the website YouTube – during which the young Keegan was asked how he'd view the prospect of moving on. He was of course nervously inarticulate compared to the way he is now, his Yorkshire accent more pronounced, but he had already learnt the art of pleasing his employers while alerting future ones: he stated that he was happy where he was, but was ambitious.

All the same, Keegan spent longer at Scunthorpe than a talented young player might reasonably expect to these days. In his debut season of 1968–69 he played twenty-nine games and another four as substitute; the following year he appeared in all forty-six, then forty-five the year after that.

That meant three years and 124 League games, taking him to the age of twenty, and little seemed to be happening for him. Millwall had made a tentative offer after a Cup game against Scunthorpe but, like the Arsenal interest, it came to nothing. Keegan grew frustrated. He was working hard; two afternoons a week he was doing as team-mate Derek Hempstead, running up and down the stand with weights to strengthen his leg muscles. He was eager to step up.

In an echo of later events, Keegan told club coach Jack Brownsword that he was thinking of quitting. Despite being something he had coveted just a few years earlier, the prospect now of a lower-division life on poor money was no longer inspiring to this thrusting character bent on self-improvement. He was weary of borrowing money from his mum and dad, as he did to upgrade a banger of a Morris to a Ford Cortina. He would later admit that he probably wouldn't have quit, but even at that early age Keegan was illustrating his propensity to respond emotionally and hastily when depressed.

Towards the end of the 1970–71 season Preston North End, through their manager, Alan Ball Senior, made a £27,500 offer for Keegan but to his annoyance Scunthorpe held out for £32,500 and Preston were turned down.

Mark Lawrenson, who went on to play for Liverpool and the Republic of Ireland, was then a junior at Preston, and his stepfather was on the board at Deepdale. 'He told me they just couldn't afford the extra five grand for Kevin,' Lawrenson recalls. What might have been, for both Keegan and Proud Preston. (Or Once-Proud Preston, as they came to be known after their decline.) Instead, another club stepped in, changing lives and the English game.

Mighty Liverpool had no such money worries and now decided to take a chance while others were dithering. Bill Shankly was an old Preston man himself and had employed a former team-mate called Andy Beattie as a scout. Beattie kept telling him about this kid named Keegan. Shankly's assistant, Bob Paisley, had also seen Keegan playing in a Cup tie on Merseyside, at Birkenhead against Tranmere Rovers, and urged Shankly to sign him.

'At that time I think Liverpool had an end-of-season policy, that Bill Shankly would get out and spend any money rather than give it to the tax man, and Kevin was taken on,' says Lawrie McMenemy.

After a medical, Keegan talked terms with Shankly; no agent then to extract maximum value. At a time when Keegan was getting £25 a week, Shankly offered him £45. Keegan was just about to take it but blurted out that he was getting £35 a week at Scunthorpe and was hoping for a bit more. Shankly made it a round £50, which Keegan took with glee.

Soon came the bonus. Shankly also offered £100 per first-team appearance; he was of the mind that if Keegan made it through he'd deserve to get what the club's top men were making, competition being so fierce at Anfield. He added that Keegan would never again need to ask for a pay-rise because he would be well rewarded.

'He believed that if you were good enough to sign for Liverpool, you deserved to be paid the going rate,' Keegan later said. 'That was something I carried with me into management. I didn't want cheap labour and if a player was worth more than I was paying him I would tear up his contract and pay him more.'

Keegan's grounding in the nether regions of the game was complete. Now began one of the great relationships of the English game, one that would cast a long and glorious shadow over it for the next forty years. After Sister Mary Oliver, Kevin Keegan had found a second mentor who would inform the rest of his life.

3

The Kop

Contrary to the insistence of misty memories that it was the best of times for the red half of Merseyside when, in that summer of 1971, Kevin Keegan arrived in Liverpool and Anfield, he entered neither a upbeat city nor an especially successful football club.

The sixties had been good to the city. As frustrated teenagers growing up in the provinces would probably testify, the supposed sexual revolution had been confined mainly to London. So it was via another aspect of the social and cultural changes that the country was undergoing that Liverpool came to the attention of the world: the vibrant music scene. The Mersey Beat, with the Cavern Club at its hub, was led by the Beatles and followed by a mass of other groups. World domination followed and the historical legacy remains intact today.

In 1963 – the year in which sex was invented, according to the poet Philip Larkin – Gerry Marsden and his band the Pacemakers had had a huge Number 1 hit with their pop version of the Rodgers and Hammerstein show ballad 'You'll

Never Walk Alone', from *Carousel*. It was at the time the Anfield custom to play the week's top record right before the teams ran out on to the pitch. The DJ received so many requests for this song, however, long after it had been knocked off the top spot in the charts, that it was played week after week, game after game, and eventually became accepted as the team's run-out music and the club's theme tune.

The sentimental anthem caught perfectly the mood of the city, at the time and many others. It told of hard times but also of huge dignity and optimism. Dreams may be tossed and blown but at the end of the storm was a golden sky and a sweet silver song. Its swelling emotionalism could be sung by a huge chorus of people who felt deeply for their club and city; it was appropriate to both triumph and tragedy.

Hard as it may be to imagine now, in April 1959 a Second Division Liverpool had attracted only 11,976 to a League game against Scunthorpe United. Bill Shankly arrived as manager in December that year and turned the club around. Within three seasons Liverpool FC was a powerhouse and had won promotion; the Football League Championship followed in 1964.

The Spion Kop, named after a South African hill from the Boer War, moved with the music and was moved by its football, growing famous as a swaying, braying mass of humanity and inhuman acts, such as urinating where you stood or in a neighbour's pocket.

Seats may now have replaced the terracing, with the atmosphere consequently diluted, but still on grey winter days Liverpool's shirts seem scarlet rather than merely red and the opening bars of the club anthem still make the hairs on the back of the neck stand up. Nowadays the atmosphere at only one other English football club can rival that of Anfield, and that club is not Manchester United – certainly not now they've adopted and adapted silly American tunes like 'Take Me Home, Country Roads' – nor is it Arsenal, nor Chelsea. It is Newcastle United, if and when they play that Mark Knopfler tune 'Coming Home'.

The music had by no means died by 1971 but it was certainly much quieter around Merseyside as more pap – in the form of glam rock – than pop was breaking through. Harold Wilson's Labour government had been ousted the previous year, to be replaced by Ted Heath's Conservatives. As the docks all but disappeared and Cammell Laird shipbuilders struggled on the Birkenhead side, unemployment under Margaret Thatcher's reign began to rise towards the worrying levels that eventually became desperate and depressing, frightening even, and prompted Alan Bleasdale to write his touchstone drama *Boys from the Black Stuff* a decade later.

At such times, almost perversely, football often prospers as the escapism of the disenfranchised working man, who makes financial cut-backs in other areas of life so long as there's just enough to get to the game. Back then, too, in the days of terracing, watching football was more affordable, less aggressively commercial, and all the more so at Liverpool. The club was controlled by the benevolently patrician Moores family, who owned the Littlewoods pools and mail-order empire chaired by Sir John Moores. The Moores were even known to reduce season-ticket prices for the season following a club profit.

This attitude was perhaps why Liverpool began to be left behind financially in the 1990s, despite their towering position in the European game. As the Premier League took off, and television money added to new sponsorship and merchandising opportunities, the club fell significantly short of others, predominantly Manchester United and Arsenal.

To put it charitably, the club was unwilling to fleece their loyal, less-moneyed fans. Though there were certainly numbers from Ireland and the shires, Liverpool's fans came mainly from within the city, rather than from far-flung corners of England – as is the case with, say, Manchester United's support. Nonetheless Liverpool were also guilty of missing the commercial boat because of complacency and indolence in their administration. As a result of this the heir to the now less lucrative Littlewoods concern, David Moores, eventually felt that he needed to sell out in a new millennium to raise investment elsewhere, thus opening up the hornet's nest that became the club's fractious American ownership involving George Gillett and Tom Hicks.

Long before the economic revolution, in the days when clubs with fan bases could still seek to do more than simply survive, and in fact could come up from the Second Division to challenge the top clubs, Shankly was the architect of a playing revolution. He understood implicitly the supporters and their aspirations. The son of a miner from Glenbuck in Ayrshire, he was both fierce Socialist and muscular Christian. For a while, after his retirement from Liverpool, he hosted a programme on Merseyside's Radio City and there conducted an interview with an awestruck former prime minister Harold Wilson. He asked Wilson who had been the first modern Socialist; Wilson offered Ramsay MacDonald.

'No,' Shankly countered. 'Jesus Christ, son, Jesus Christ.'

Shankly so badly wanted to deliver to his public, these people. And when he did, in winning the 1974 FA Cup, his whole credo emerged in a stirring speech delivered to a gathering of 80,000 in St George's Square.

'Since I've come here to Liverpool, to Anfield, I've drummed it into my players time and time again that they are privileged to play for you,' he said to rousing cheers. 'And if they didn't believe me then, they do now. I've drummed into them that they must be loyal, that they must never cheat you the public.

'The Kop's exclusive, an institution, and if you're a member of the Kop, you feel you're a member of a society. You've got thousands of friends around you and they're united and loyal.'

This climactic speech would be one of the last acts of Shankly's astonishing, silver-strewn career. In 1971, however, when he signed Keegan, he was still searching for a new perfect blend. For Liverpool had not won a trophy since 1966, with the League Championship that May coming just ahead of England's World Cup win. His great team was now breaking up, a fact signalled to him by an FA Cup defeat at Watford in the February of 1970, and he needed to rebuild.

Ian St John, for example, was already sold to Coventry City. As reinforcement in attack that summer, a year ahead of Keegan's arrival, Shankly paid Cardiff City £180,000 for a lanky, powerful striker called John Toshack. Yet still something was not quite right in the absence of a St John-style player, someone smaller and nippier. Liverpool finished fifth in the League; and, having beaten neighbours Everton in the semi-final, lost a marvellous, memorable FA Cup Final 2–1 to Arsenal, who completed the Double with the victory.

Keegan had signed for Liverpool in the week of that Cup Final. He was included in the party that stayed at the Waldorf Hotel in London, but he was there for the ride and the experience – was never really a part of it. It was the Liverpool way, then a mixture of carrot and stick. There was a tantalising glimpse of the first team, but the majority had to bide their time, learn the ways of the club, before getting anywhere near.

As if to emphasise this fact, Keegan's induction continued the following week when he played a couple of games on an end-of-season tour to Scandinavia. Shankly was quick to quell any ideas above stations, though; in the 1971–72 pre-season

Keegan was packed off with the reserves while the first team went to Germany.

The seniors struggled for goals, though, and Shankly became increasingly concerned. Toshack and Alun Evans did not look like a great pairing in attack. Then the manager saw Keegan – who moved in from the right to the attack – score twice in a friendly against Southport. He was subsequently paired with Toshack for a first team versus reserves game in training and again scored twice, with the Welshman also netting a hat-trick.

Shankly could not have known for sure that Keegan would fill the boots of such a Kop legend as Ian St John, especially since the kid from Scunthorpe had been playing as a right-winger, but his faith in Keegan was an example of the intuitive management that made him what he was. It was surely something that Keegan under different circumstances would have noted, something that would have given him food for thought; at the time, though, he was like most young players unable yet to see the bigger picture. He was just happy to be in first-team contention.

To everyone's surprise, for many on the Kop were still unaware of Keegan's name when it was read out with the rest of the team's, Shankly stuck Keegan straight in on opening day against Nottingham Forest. And he gave him an instruction that Keegan would recall and recycle for years to come:

'Just go out there and drop some hand grenades, son.'

Keegan did. In fact he scored after only twelve minutes. It

was a mis-hit shot after he had poorly controlled Peter Thompson's pass, but no matter. The Kop was chanting his name as Liverpool won 3–1. He was on his way, and he would score three times in the opening five games to cement his place.

Liverpool went on to finish third that thrilling season, in a title race that went to the last game of the season and saw Brian Clough's Derby County prevail ahead of Don Revie's second-place Leeds. But for a defeat at Derby and a draw at Arsenal in the last two games of the season, Keegan would have had a Championship medal in his first season. He had been the success of the season, though, and Liverpool were now the coming team in English football.

Keegan would not have to wait much longer for his Championship medal. As he matured, so did the team. They won the title the next season, along with the UEFA Cup, the club's first European trophy, as he doubled his goals tally from eleven to twenty-two. Indeed, he accumulated three Championships in all, along with another UEFA Cup in 1976 on top of the FA Cup of 1974, when they beat Newcastle 3–0. That was the year in which Shankly retired, to be succeeded by Bob Paisley. That season Keegan played in all sixty-one Liverpool matches and along the way twice scored against his hometown, Doncaster Rovers, after Liverpool had been trailing in a Cup tie at Anfield. He had shown Donny and Newcastle; what a triumph for him. In total, he played 323 games for Liverpool and scored exactly 100 goals in his six seasons with the club.

The crowning glory in all this was undoubtedly the European Cup of 1977, when Keegan was the inspiration for the 3–1 win in the Final over Borussia Moenchengladbach and his legendary pulling hither and thither of his marker, the tenacious Berti Vogts, the notable feature of the game.

This parade of success and achievement was based on three key elements that directed the rest of Keegan's footballing life: his relationship with Shankly, which later defined his own management style and his interaction with his players; his partnership with Toshack, which sold to him the need for a balance of strikers in a preferred 4–4–2 system; and his own phenomenal work ethic, which transformed him from a determined little winger to an outstanding, high-achieving striker.

Keegan was the missing link between the first and second great sides that Shankly – the fiercely driven Scot who paved the way for such compatriots as Sir Alex Ferguson and George Graham to succeed in England – almost chanced upon, in much the same way that Ferguson did with Eric Cantona.

Shankly immediately took to Keegan, recalling later that he 'ignited the passion'. Keegan in turn has described the day he met Shankly as 'the highlight of my life'.

The gnarled old Scot loved the infectious enthusiasm of the

kid and first saw something to inspire him on the day Liverpool lost the 1971 Cup Final to Arsenal – a day when Shankly must have had plenty of other things on his mind. Keegan was apparently distraught at the defeat and Shankly loved seeing this in a player who wasn't even in the team.

Keegan came to revere the paternal Shankly. According to Bob Harris, 'Everybody did. It wasn't difficult. Shankly was special. And he had this great ability with players of making them feel special. He was like that with Kevin straight from the start. He knew he had got something useful there.'

Keegan also came to believe and trust unreservedly everything Shankly said. 'If he told you to go to hell,' Keegan would later say, 'you'd ask what time he wanted you to leave.' The manager, for example, once told Keegan that he would soon play for England and in just over a year he did.

'Kevin is like a weasel after rats, always biting and snapping at your legs,' said Shankly. The manager also loved his boxing and was fond of an analogy. 'He's a perfect size. A fully fledged middleweight, the greatest fighter of them all.'

Shankly, indeed, was ever the most quotable and inspirational of managers, not through rehearsal but through natural wit and wisdom. This characteristic was something Keegan would later take into his own career as a leader. The sayings are legendary, though that oft-repeated one about football not being a matter of life or death, but far more important than that, was surely said tongue in cheek. Wasn't it?

There is a tale of the aftermath to the 1971 Final when

Shankly addressed the masses in Liverpool the following day: 'Yesterday at Wembley we may have lost the Cup but you the Liverpool people won everything. You have won the admiration of the policemen in London and you have won the admiration of the public in London.'

On the way, apparently, Shankly had turned to university-educated midfielder Brian Hall to ask him about 'that chairman with the red book, lots of sayings, the Chinaman'. Hall correctly suggested that he meant Chairman Mao. Soon, on the balcony of St George's Hall, Shankly had the Liverpool hordes as far as the eye could see cheering yet more when he said, 'Chairman Mao has never seen the greatest show of red strength.'

Keegan has told a story that illustrates how Shankly could make him feel ten feet tall. Against West Ham one day, Shankly informed Keegan that he had just seen the England and Hammers' captain Bobby Moore looking dreadful, that he must have been at a nightclub and wouldn't fancy playing against Liverpool that day. Keegan duly went out, played well as Liverpool won – only to be told afterwards by Shankly that Moore was quite some player.

'It was the Shanks psychology,' Keegan recalled. 'Having built me up before the match, he now praised my opponent so that I wouldn't go away thinking I had done well because of any defect of his.'

Shankly clearly regarded Keegan as his protégé and talisman, but actually this story is representative of how he behaved with all players – seeking to draw out that extra bit of performance. Indeed, he may well have been the game's first true sports psychologist, with his innate ability to discern what made players tick and thus to motivate them. And of course he had tactical and technical expertise to boot.

'He said, "Never be frightened to miss,"' John Toshack recalled, for example. '"You must always go into the penalty area. If you go in and miss one, you go in with more determination next time." I think it's probably the best bit of advice I ever had as a forward player.'

There was another, more fearsome, side to Shankly, as there is with any leader – certainly those in football, where egos and personalities clash, emotions run high and battle is hot. Steve Heighway, the former left-winger who eventually became Liverpool's Youth Academy director, admits to being frightened of Shankly.

'A lot of people see Shanks as being amusing and warm, and he was all those things,' he says. 'But I guarantee that ninety-nine per cent of the players were frightened to death of him because he had that very abrasive, aggressive side to him.' One suspects that Keegan was in the other one per cent; that 'respectful' might more adequately describe his feelings for Shankly.

Shankly threatened to quit virtually every summer, wearied by long seasons, and in need of comforting words from the board of directors to tell him how loved and valued he was and what a fine job he was doing. Then, in the summer of

1974, he told them that he meant it and was going to leave. All concerned were stunned that he could just walk away from his life's work at the age of sixty when he was still fit and healthy.

Within six weeks, however, having rested up, he regretted his decision and sought his old job back. But the die was cast. His assistant Bob Paisley had taken over his position. Shankly grew sad; he took to walking around the Melwood training ground on a daily basis, until it was subtly brought to his attention that this sort of daily visit could become embarrassing to the club and was not welcome. He began to take regular walks around Everton's Bellefield training ground instead. The whole episode was a poignant and unhappy time for the club and the great man.

In his biography of Shankly, *It's Much More Important Than That*, Stephen F. Kelly wrote: 'Shankly was a highly emotional man, torn between drama and devotion.'

There are no prizes for guessing who else might come to fit that description. The only difference appears to be that when Keegan made a decision, no matter how knee-jerk and emotional it might have seemed in hindsight, and no matter his private regret, he never went back on it. This was certainly true later in his managerial career, after his initial Newcastle experience.

'Many people have said that I was a similar manager to Shankly and copied his techniques,' Keegan has said. 'I would have been a fool not to have taken his strong points on board.

For me the entire purpose of meeting people is to learn something from them, whether it is positive or negative.

'There was an awful lot to learn from Shanks but what you couldn't copy was the aura he created and built up over the years. And the trust the fans had in him: you could try to earn that but you couldn't come anywhere near it. It all had to be there from the start, not simply the passion but the control of the passion.

'He was much better at controlling his passion and hiding his tension than I was. The greatest thing I took from him to Newcastle was the belief that a football club is for the fans. It is sad that the game has changed so much that players can no longer go and have a drink with the supporters because of an us-and-them situation. Shanks crossed that barrier with ease.'

Keegan also considers himself more tolerant than Shankly and his approach to injured players perhaps reflects this difference in temperament. Shankly would barely nod in acknowledgement of players who were injured. 'Didn't want to talk to them,' says Bob Harris. 'Anyone with a tracksuit bottom on, "Don't want him on my training pitch."' Indeed, he once told iron defender Tommy Smith to remove what he considered to be an effeminate bandage from his knee. That knee belonged to Liverpool, Shankly said. Keegan later proved himself to be rather less ruthless in this respect.

Keegan has confessed that some of his depth of feeling for Liverpool FC went with the departure of his guru. That may be so, but he always gave of his best and respected Paisley, an unassuming man who never seemed to want the job (according to Harris, Paisley was often to be seen in hotel lobbies on Liverpool trips abroad, reading a book and wearing his slippers) but achieved astounding success. Keegan's professionalism was unquestionable; that and his desire to ride the wave of popularity and commercial success now coming his way.

He had forged an extraordinary partnership with John Toshack, who, strange as it may seem now, was not always Shankly's favourite. Shankly often dropped Toshack from the team – even tried unsuccessfully to buy Frank Worthington from Leicester as a replacement. When Shankly decided to leave Toshack out for a European Cup tie against Borussia Moenchgladbach, Toshack contemplated a transfer request. Shankly had second thoughts and played him; he and Keegan duly prospered and the game was won.

'Myself and Kevin Keegan worked up a good understanding and as a partnership we flourished,' Toshack has said. 'We seemed to hit it off from almost day one and then got better and better as time went by.'

Said Keegan, for his part: 'Toshack was a wonderful player to play alongside. His aerial ability was fantastic and I always knew that he was going to win the high balls. From then on, it was just a question of me reading which way the ball was going to go and from those situations we created many chances. I always admired Tosh's honesty as a player.'

They were much in demand off the pitch, too, and were

pictured together as Batman and Robin. Toshack even wrote a book of poetry entitled *Gosh it's Tosh,* which featured the memorable stanza:

> Coming in to land at Speke,
> My legs are feeling very weak,
> We've just returned from Barcelona,
> And now I'm going for a sauna.

It passed into the game's folklore that the duo had a telepathic understanding and a television company had the idea of testing them to see if they could read what cards were in each other's hand. The results were astonishing. That is, until Keegan later revealed that they'd used mirrors.

Keegan also had an amazing work ethic and became celebrated for making himself into an effective and successful player through his industry, both in the sense of working at his game and in the amount of ground he covered.

'He made himself a great player,' says Bobby Robson. 'He had a great urge and great ambition to maximise what he had with his bravery and reading of the game.

'Toshack and Keegan were great foils, weren't they? Tosh used to flick it on and the kid was on his way. He thought that Toshack would win the ball and took a gamble. He kept onside and timed his runs well. Toshack was a big lad and good in the air, Keegan a brisk player with a bit of pace and liveliness in his game.

'He was zippy, a darting little player who would stick his head in because he was only pint-sized. He went in on challenges and picked himself up again, never did the diving and rolling. If you are playing at the highest level and you are that small, you have got to have some qualities otherwise you get buried.'

Tony Adams, who years later captained England under Keegan, played against him just once and it stuck in his mind. It was in 1988, in Cyprus, when Arsenal were on an end-of-season tour and playing against a Celebrity XI that featured Keegan, who was by then living in Spain and making the odd guest appearance for various sides.

'People say about him, fairly or unfairly, that he made himself a player, that it was his effort and work-rate and I certainly noticed that in that game,' says Adams. 'He worked his socks off. What was he, thirty-seven? I couldn't believe the amount of effort and energy he put into an exhibition game.

'As a kid growing up and wanting to play the game, I was very much aware of him – though I never had heroes, really. I knew the man was very focussed and very determined, very compact, very strong. He was also in a fantastic team and worked hard to get himself and them a lot of success so I can identify with him in that.'

Adds Rogan Taylor, academic and Liverpool fan through five decades: 'He was never a Pele or a Cruyff. Shankly helped him to become a great footballer. For the Kop, it is a key subcultural value that you can get away with virtually anything if you give everything; and he showed great effort, working unselfishly with Toshack. He was also great in the air for a small man, like Ian St John.'

Not everyone rated him so highly. With a touch of envy, perhaps – not at the talent but at the way Keegan had business savvy and knew how to hold on to his money – George Best described him as 'very, very lucky – an average player who came into the game when it was short of personalities. He's not fit to lace my boots as a player.' The perceptive sportswriter John Roberts, of the *Guardian* and the *Independent*, once memorably wrote that Keegan was not fit to lace Best's drinks.

So Keegan with all his qualities continued to devote himself to the Liverpool cause following Shankly's departure. Nonetheless he was clearly not happy that summer of 1974, despite having just won the FA Cup – recognised as more of an achievement then than it is now – after scoring twice in the 3–0 win over Newcastle. It's possible that his mood had something to do with England's failure to qualify for the World Cup finals in West Germany that year.

On a pre-season tour of Germany he was sent off for kicking a Kaiserslautern player in retaliation for a bad tackle on Ray Kennedy, Shankly's last signing before resigning and new to the club. He escaped any punishment, however, when the club claimed that the miscreant had been Peter Cormack, who had similar long hair and sideburns, the fashion of the time.

This being in the days before every game, including pre-season friendlies, was shown on television, the confusion was such that both men got away with it.

Keegan was not so lucky four days later. It was Leeds versus Liverpool in the FA Charity Shield, now named the Community Shield, the pre-season showpiece featuring the League champions and FA Cup winners. In this instance the rivalry between the participating clubs was one of the most memorable of the seventies; it was a massive clash with no love lost. In fact, at the time, nobody wasted love on Leeds.

In the finale to a series of nasty tackles and incidents, Keegan traded punches with the feisty, fiery redheaded Scot Billy Bremner, embodiment of all that was rugged and mistrusted about Leeds, and both were sent off to provide the papers with screaming headlines. Both men would be banned for a draconian eleven games.

'He had this spark, this fierce little temperament,' says Bob Harris, who was watching up in the press box that day. 'It was shown with that clash. Looking back, I think it was one of the all-time funny stories, though it was pretty serious at the time. Imagine that today – somebody getting sent off in the Community Shield. But it was Bremner and Keegan. It was rare for Kevin. He wasn't an undisciplined player or person.'

Keegan has said that to this day he does not know why he reacted so. What with Germany and Wembley on top, a mixture of anger and grief at the loss of Shankly might well also have contributed. There was even uncertainty around the club, with talk of Paisley being a mere stopgap and Brian Clough's possible arrival.

'Like the rain in Manchester, though the rain in Manchester stops sometimes,' Shankly had said of Clough in that wonderful era when managers were becoming characters and had thus begun to trade insults by means to getting the psychological upper hand. Later we would see Keegan and Sir Alex Ferguson indulging in spats as precursor to Ferguson and Arsene Wenger; then Ferguson and Wenger and Jose Mourinho.

In 1977, though, Paisley would achieve something that Shankly could not – Shankly's one regret, he said in his final press conference – by winning the European Cup. The win provided the fairytale ending to Keegan's career with the club: Liverpool beat Moenchengladbach; Keegan created the sealing goal, by racing into the penalty area and luring Berti Vogts into bringing him down.

'Vogts was the Claude Makelele of his day and he ran him ragged,' says Rogan Taylor. 'The penalty was almost a kind of tribute from him to Keegan.'

It was Keegan's last act in his last game for Liverpool. He had told the club the previous summer that he would give it one more season then wanted to try his hand abroad. Cannily, he had a clause in his contract allowing him to leave for a transfer fee of £500,000.

This may have been pre-Jean Marc Bosman, the Belgian

who tested and changed European law governing the free movement of players at the end of their contracts, but Keegan was certainly shrewd. He knew that the lower the fee, the more a prospective club would be willing to shell out in wages – this being the accepted modern principle for players whose contracts are running down.

In the seventies this was a controversial decision – revolutionary, almost – and one that divided opinion in the city. There were even mixed feelings among some of those who had always seen Keegan as an untainted hero. It was an example of what Bob Harris came to notice about Keegan:

'He was – how to phrase this properly? – selfish and self-centred are perhaps not the right words but he was very much his own man. He knew what he wanted to do and how he was going to do it and would fight for that.'

Many on Merseyside felt it an affront that any player would want to leave Liverpool. As a result Keegan did not enjoy quite the worshipful send-off he might otherwise have been given – though his finale was a glorious one, Liverpool having won the League title and the European Cup Final and failing with an astonishing treble only because they lost the FA Cup final to Manchester United just four days before the latter victory.

Keegan had known that Liverpool stood a good chance of winning the European Cup that season and this was one of the reasons why he'd informed the club ahead of time of his intention to move abroad. The club was a remarkably civilised, benign organisation in those days and he did a deal with Liverpool's then chairman, Sir John Smith: Keegan would see the year through, giving his all; in return the club would not price him out of the market.

For all that, the arrangement he negotiated would be almost unthinkable and unworkable now, when a player in his position would surely be shipped out immediately his intentions became clear. Such is the business culture of the game, with clubs seeking to cash in on the player as asset in case of injury and/or fading form. Some twenty-five years after Keegan's departure from Liverpool, Michael Owen left the club for Real Madrid at the height of the transfer market for what was the knock-down price of £15million – with one year of his contract remaining.

Naturally Keegan's deal became public knowledge and many Liverpool fans were unhappy with his decision, believing him to be less effective that season than previously. (This despite his goals records holding up: the twenty he scored made it the second-best return of his career with the club.) That said, while there was even then a vigilant press, football news was covered less than it is now on television and radio and the focus on the game was not as intense, more tolerant. The disgruntlement was always contained in a way it would not be now, when there are radio phone-ins and internet message-boards to contend with.

All the same, the circumstance of his departure may well factor in why the Kop never quite hold Keegan in the esteem reserved for its most favoured sons. In a poll in 2006 he was voted Number 8 in the Top 100 Liverpool players of all time. Given his impact and achievements, and his six-year stay, he might have expected to be higher.

'A lot of people liked and admired him, even loved him for what he had given the cause,' says Rogan Taylor, a long-standing Koppite. 'When it came to the big games, he never hid or failed to show.

'What I liked about him was the honesty of his football. He looked more like a Rugby League player because he was stocky but small, but he overcame that with the most fantastic application and tremendous bravery, along with tremendous pace.

'He got whacked by centre-halves but I never saw him stay down unless he was being carried off. He bounced up like a tennis ball.'

Taylor refutes the suggestion that Keegan was not fully firing in his final season. 'That impression came from habit or expectation rather than the reality,' he says. 'I don't recollect ever coming away from a game thinking, "Keegan did nothing today."'

Taylor does remember taking issue with certain fellow Koppites who were less than generous towards Keegan on his last appearance at Anfield, in May 1977, at home to West Ham, with Liverpool just having been crowned champions.

'I remember at the time getting pissed off that he was not getting the recognition from some on the Kop of what a great footballer he was. In fact, I remember turning round and speaking to some Scousers who were not giving him a better time.'

He also understands, however, where the ultimately qualified sense of affection came from. 'People wondered where he was going from Liverpool. Players came for ten years, played, stayed and retired. Tommy Smith was there for twenty years. Later in his management jobs he became imperially twitchy, didn't he? Perhaps Scousers saw something of that before everyone else.'

Taylor identifies what some on Merseyside, where commercial profit from the game was seen as somehow distasteful, may also have felt about Keegan the superstar – who was by this time highly sought after for advertising and endorsements.

'He had a commercial nous coupled with self-absorption that just stops you falling in love with him,' is how Taylor puts it.

Either way, in the habit that football has of quickly moving on, it became a case of 'The King is dead, long live the King'. Liverpool signed Kenny Dalglish from Celtic as Keegan's replacement for £440,000 and within a year he had brought them another European Cup with a winning goal against Bruges at Wembley.

'It was ironic,' says Taylor. 'Kevin worked at being a great player and was the door to Kenny, who was the most naturally gifted player in a red shirt I ever saw.'

*

Actually, it all almost backfired on Keegan that final season. Throughout the year there was much talk of the big European clubs taking him, but the glamorous clubs of Spain did not see him as an exotic enough talent while the technicians of Italy were apparently undecided.

The more functional German clubs were the ones most attracted and it was Hamburger Sport Verein who put the money where their mouth was. Bayern Munich did make a late enquiry but it came to Keegan personally and not to Liverpool, as it should have done, and was brushed off. Keegan finally did the deal with Hamburg on the eve of the FA Cup Final lost to Manchester United. His renaissance in the European Cup Final against Borussia Moenchengladbach may well have had something to do with being settled at last, and with wanting to impress against a club in whose country he would be plying his trade.

German football in those days was rich and well supported commercially and Hamburg had made quite an offer – the likes of which would not be seen nowadays, when German salaries offer little to tempt an Englishman who knows on which side his *Brot* is buttered. Keegan would be getting a basic salary of £100,000 a year – four times his Liverpool wage at that time. Now, that sort of multiplication is more likely to apply to players coming from Hamburg to Liverpool.

He would be going from an English port to a German port, to a country that, appropriately for Keegan, valued and rewarded industry, consistency and mental toughness.

4

Coast to Coast

The geography of European football was considerably different in 1977 from the landscape now dominated by the power of players. Long before the Champions League, long before the Bosman case that enabled footballers to move freely at the end of their contracts and long before the European Union declared free movement of labour, players from England rarely travelled abroad.

In the fifties the great Welshman John Charles, quite probably Britain's most underrated player ever, went from Leeds to Juventus, while in the sixties Jimmy Greaves moved from Chelsea to Milan and Denis Law from Manchester City to Torino, but these were all isolated events and the latter two were not great successes.

Kevin Keegan, by now the English game's biggest star, ever ambitious and eager for self-improvement, would blaze a trail. After him, in the eighties and nineties, there would be plenty of examples – Ray Wilkins, Mark Hateley, Trevor Francis, Ian Rush, David Platt and Paul Gascoigne moving to Italy, even Tony Woodcock going to Germany, from

Nottingham Forest to Cologne – until the arrival of the vast sums on offer as the Premier League grew and fewer wanted or needed to go abroad.

Keegan's move to Hamburg certainly offers a glimpse at what is now thought of as a golden era, though interestingly those who lived through it may recall much hooliganism, cynicism and low-scoring games on poor pitches in inadequate stadiums. But it is intriguing in another respect also: that being as a formative experience in Keegan's development both personally and professionally in advance of his managerial career. His departure from Liverpool was not smooth; and nor was his docking in 'the Venice of Northern Europe', on the River Elbe between the North and Baltic seas.

With his wife, Jean, who had studied A level German at school, Keegan endured a gloomy introduction to Hamburg city and the club, as they – with two Old English Sheepdogs in tow – were billeted on the nineteenth floor of a high-rise hotel before they found a house in the country.

Keegan was being hailed as the club's saviour by its business manager, Dr Peter Krohn, which was odd considering that they had just beaten Ajax to win the European Cup-Winners' Cup. Krohn also shouted Keegan's salary from the rooftops.

It was the highest wage in Germany, topping £130,000 with bonuses. After tax it was worth £70,000 to him, whereas at Liverpool he had taken home £12,000 – but much of his money was coming from commercial endorsements, including advertising and boot deals. All in, he would earn £250,000 annually, channelled through his company on the tax-efficient Isle of Man, which set him on the way to becoming the first English footballing millionaire.

Not that it was all money with him, though he was always open to deals that his agent in England, Harry Swales, might put to him. Keegan was capable of making generous gestures – as had been Shankly, who would personally supply worthy causes with Cup Final tickets on the quiet.

At his own expense Keegan returned to Anfield later that first season to play in a testimonial for the Liverpool full-back Chris Lawler. Shankly spoke to him afterwards with a splendid, characteristic piece of carrot and stick.

'Jesus Christ, you've climbed Everest, son,' he said. 'Now see if you can stay there.'

Keegan's Hamburg team-mates were on far less money and were jealous. His very presence was also questioned since he was replacing a popular Dutchman, Horst Blankenberg. At the time only two overseas players were permitted in any one *Bundesliga* team, the other in this instance being Ivan Buljan, a Yugoslav.

The club was riven by politics and the team began the season badly, results including a 6–0 defeat at Liverpool – which was personally embarrassing to Keegan – in the second leg of the European Super Cup. Krohn and the coach Rudi Gutendorf were sacked, leaving a still-settling Keegan slightly baffled by it all but concentrating on his game. In came

Gunter Netzer, the West German midfield legend, to steady the ship.

It was significant that Keegan emerged from the political and economic shenanigans with his own reputation and form intact. He learnt the language intently and his progress in this was helped by the fact that he was living in a rural area, where few spoke English, and so was forced to practise. By October, he had won the German equivalent of the Goal of the Month competition and was conducting television interviews in the language. Keegan's fierce pride, determination to succeed and avoid ridicule back home were seeing him through. They would do again the following year when a Yugoslav, the staunch disciplinarian Branco Zelec, took over as coach and Netzer became general manager.

Once Keegan got over his initial discomfort, his three-season sojourn became an astonishing personal triumph. Hamburg finished sixth, then became champions and were subsequently runners-up. Mainly on the back of his European Cup Final performance for Liverpool, he had been runner-up to the Dane Allan Simonsen as European Player of the Year in 1977. In 1978 and 1979 he won the honour, which was an incredible achievement for an Englishman – at the time such players as Johan Cruyff, Franz Beckenbauer and Michel Platini were around, after all – and one that has not since been emulated. Keegan also led Hamburg to the 1980 European Cup Final, where they lost 1–0 to Brian Clough's Nottingham Forest.

Keegan did encounter lack of success with a song he

recorded, 'Head Over Heels in Love', which reached only Number 31 in the British charts, though it did bring him an appearance on *Top of the Pops* and hit Number 10 in Germany, where traditionally attitudes to pop music have been more forgiving, less discerning perhaps. His follow-up, 'To Be Home Again in England', proved popular with exiles on the BBC Radio Sunday-morning show *Family Favourites*.

That apart, Keegan drew much admiration, mostly for his football but also for the way he embraced and enjoyed German life. He was awarded the affectionate nickname *Machtig Maus* – Mighty Mouse – after the cartoon character of that name. A boxer, a Rugby League player, a mouse . . . Now Uwe Seeler, Hamburg legend and captain of the 1970 West German World Cup semi-finalists who had beaten England, compared him with a little Volkswagen, nippy and reliable.

Keegan's popularity was sealed when he agreed to extend his contract to a third year when he could have gone to Spain or Italy, with Barcelona, Real Madrid and Juventus now taking an interest. Though Keegan never warmed to him – probably because Bill Shankly was suspicious of a big rival – Brian Clough even asked him if he fancied Nottingham Forest. At the time the pair were on the ITV World Cup panel of 1978. The approach came in the gents toilets at London Weekend Television.

Although, in hindsight, he might have become a European champion again had he agreed to the move, there was method in Keegan's decision to stay on at Hamburg. It was not just because Hamburg themselves were now in the European Cup and he thought they had a good chance, the situation he had been in at Liverpool. The Germans would also allow him to play a summer in America for the Washington Diplomats, for an enormous £250,000. Unfortunately for them, Hamburg were then informed of a rule that if he did so he would be ineligible for the European Cup the following season until the semi-finals. Staggeringly, Hamburg paid him the sum for cancelling the contract with Washington.

In return Keegan agreed to advertise their sponsors, BP. Thus was Keegan, his face framed by the fashionable bubble-perm, already well known on billboards and TV, at the forefront of a new strategy of commercial activity that later saw Gary Lineker then David Beckham become the faces of companies. This coincided with advancements in commercialism because of the increasing prevalence of colour television and put Keegan at the vanguard yet again.

The back-scratching continued when Hamburg, as Liverpool had done before, agreed to a transfer fee of a maximum of £500,000 – testimony to his power in the game.

When he began, midway through his third season at Hamburg, to consider his next move, Italy appeared to be the favoured destination and Juventus in particular were making noises. But Keegan and Jean by now had a daughter, Laura, and news stories about kidnapping worried his wife. She wanted to go back to England.

Lawrie McMenemy, charismatic Geordie, big of stature and personality, manager of Southampton, was taking note. And he had a fanciful notion of pulling off one of the biggest transfer coups ever in the English game.

'I was amazed that Kevin had to win them over in Germany,' he says. 'There was a story that they wouldn't even pass the ball to him. Now ninety-nine people out of a hundred away from home would have crumbled. But he didn't. He just rolled up his sleeves that bit further. Not only did he win his team-mates over but the whole of Europe, not once but twice. So I am watching all this and admiring him.

'Then I read that Kevin Keegan was likely to move on at the end of the season. It is commonplace now for that to happen but in those days if a fella had a contract, everyone including managers hoped that it would get renewed at the end of that contract. All the club had to do was offer the same money and he was retained, unless you got a free transfer. In Europe it was not unknown that they would move but our mentality was that you stay. At that time, he could have taken his pick.'

Just before Christmas, McMenemy found a good excuse to ring Keegan, having secured a phone number easily enough from the BBC, where he was then a leading member of their football pundits' panels, notably for World Cups.

'At the time, I had bought a plot of land to build a new house and it was just about completed. The architect loved lights and described a light he said would really finish off the staircase. The trouble was, he said, you only get it in Germany and there was a waiting list. I asked where and he said Hamburg. I said, "Give me the brochure." I was looking for a way and that sparked the way.

'I rang Kevin up and he seemed to know who I was, though I had never met him. We started having this chat. I told him about the house and the light and asked him if he could pick one up and bring it over with him next time he came back to play for England. He said, "No problem."

'I made some more calls to him to talk about the light. Then I started to ask him about the family and Germany, the baby. I eventually plucked up enough courage, eventually getting to the main point of the process, and said, "I saw something about you moving on at some stage," and told him that he was always welcome at Southampton. He didn't laugh it off.'

Indeed, the suggestion planted a seed for Keegan. He loved the New Forest and his old England mates Mick Channon and Alan Ball, with whom he shared a love of horseracing, were at the club. Keegan had done the big-club scene, won all the big prizes, and somehow fancied the idea now of being the big fish in the small pool. Southampton had won the FA Cup as a Second Division side and won promotion. Now they were stepping up a level. Keegan always loved the idea of being the leading light – as long as he had quality and resources around him and had a chance of success.

He told McMenemy that he would be willing to talk

about it with him, that he'd be over to play for England on 6 February in a European Championship qualifying match against the Republic of Ireland at Wembley. McMenemy went to his finance director, Guy Askham, swore him to secrecy and asked him to arrange a private venue for a meeting between two easily spotted and well-known men. McMenemy was by then not only a TV pundit but also the face of adverts for Barbican alcohol-free lager.

Askham had a discreet friend who owned a house in Kensington, London, and fixed up a meeting with Keegan for the Monday on his way from Heathrow to join the England squad.

'We talked about football and I was thinking, "This is a forlorn hope, but here we go,"' says McMenemy. 'I started painting a picture, talked about Mick Channon and Alan Ball, who were old friends of his. I forget how far we got in with it before Kevin said, "Have you got a contract?" and I looked at Guy, who had come with me because it wasn't straightforward – what with Kevin living abroad and the tax matters and because we didn't have much scope at all financially.

'My man said he had brought a contract and Kevin said, "Well, give it me; have you got a pen?" And he signed a blank contract. I said, "I can't believe that."' Keegan, just a week short of his twenty-ninth birthday, agreed a three-year deal.

'Then he said, "I've got something to tell you,"' adds McMenemy. '"I've forgotten your light."'

McMenemy apparently said something along the lines of

'to heck with the light' – though Keegan did eventually ensure that he got it.

Both men agreed to keep the deal quiet for the time being and began five days of excited, clandestine preparation for the transfer announcement. Keegan went off to captain England and scored both goals, the second a marvellous chip, in a 2–0 win over the Republic, then headed back to Germany to tell his manager, Gunter Netzer, what was happening. Guy Askham had to phone the Liverpool secretary, Peter Robinson, to seek permission for the signing, since Liverpool had first refusal on him coming back to England. With Anfield still purring over Kenny Dalglish, they passed. McMenemy prepared his team to face Brighton and Hove Albion on the Saturday.

After the game, with everyone in good spirits after a 5–1 win, the manager met with his board to tell them whom he was signing for the following season, having by now agreed a fee of around £400,000 with Hamburg. The manager's stock was high and he knew it would be a rubber-stamping exercise – a courtesy call, really. The board mostly comprised old-style patrician football people. Among their number were Sir George Meyrick, a local landowner who had been at Eton with the Cobbolds and Hill-Woods, who controlled Ipswich Town and Arsenal respectively; George Reader, English referee of the decisive 1950 World Cup match between Uruguay and Brazil, was also formerly a member.

'Sir George was very money-conscious and whenever there was a vote when I wanted to sign a player, he kept his hand down,' McMenemy recalls. 'With Keegan, even his hand went up. It was the only time.'

In the context of today's climate, in which it is club owners and chief executives who call the shots, McMenemy's clout in terms of doing such a deal personally, as a manager, seems unthinkable – as Keegan would discover himself one day. Not only that, but it is barely believable that all concerned were able to keep the deal quiet until it was finally made public knowledge to great astonishment.

McMenemy was sitting on the biggest story for many years – something akin to, say, David Beckham agreeing before the 2006 World Cup to leave Real Madrid for Portsmouth – but had to resist any excited urges to share the news. 'I was single-minded because I did not want a thing to spoil it,' he says.

On the Sunday night, McMenemy and his wife, Anne, had dinner with the author Leslie Thomas and his wife at their Hampshire home. McMenemy admits to being twitchy; Thomas sensed that a signing was in the offing and pressed him on the subject. Eventually, as he was leaving, McMenemy uttered, 'K. K.' The writer supposed that the Norwich City goalkeeper Kevin Keelan was signing for the Saints.

Earlier that evening, McMenemy had also called the Press Association to tell them of a planned press conference at the Potter's Heron hotel near his Romsey home the following morning. The PA in turn alerted the national newspapers, who duly gathered expectantly.

'The chairman, Alan Woodford, was with me and Alan Ball as well,' McMenemy recalls. 'I think Bally thought it was *This Is Your Life* for him, bless him. Some thought it was a new stadium, others thought I was moving, because I had had some offers. Nobody guessed.

'There was a door in the corner of the room and in walked Kevin with the baby, his wife Jean and his agent, Harry Swales, who had picked him up at Southampton airport, along with Gunter Netzer. The press stood up and applauded. At that moment I knew we had done it. He was brilliant with the media, as he has been all his career.'

This scenario, too, would be unimaginable in the modern media age. Now, there would be someone media-savvy at an airport or hotel ready to tip off a newspaper for a fee; someone taking a picture on their mobile phone, someone posting it on the internet.

Keegan returned to Germany to see the season through with Hamburg but this time there was to be no fairytale ending for him. Hamburg lost that European Cup Final to Forest and also finished runners-up in their league.

Back in England, excitement at Keegan's return went beyond Southampton, the club being inundated with mail. 'Boxes full,' says McMenemy. 'Including estate agents. Jean came over and she and Anne sifted through them, made appointments as Mrs Smith and Mrs Jones to go and see them all. At first they rented one near Stockbridge then moved into one near Romsey.

'The impact on football in general was amazing,' McMenemy adds. 'Managers were ringing me up and saying, "It's not really true, is it? Well done, congratulations." One of the first people to ring me was Arthur Cox, who I had known at Halifax. He idolised Kevin, you could tell.

'We hadn't put the cost of season tickets up for a number of years but we doubled them and got not one complaint.'

At the Dell was witnessed a remarkable period that would even carry early echoes of what Keegan would go on to establish at Newcastle. Of McMenemy, Keegan would come to say: 'He took on everything at the club, much as I did in my early days at Newcastle, but his strengths did not lie in holding training sessions or tactical awareness – although he could hold his own there. His talents were man-motivation and a sharp eye.'

Southampton became a freewheeling, attractive, attacking team, with McMenemy having decided upon a combination of young players gathered via a scouting network he had established in such places as the North East, which would post-Keegan produce Alan Shearer for the club, and the Channel Islands (Matthew Le Tissier) and wily old talented players, among them Channon, Ball and Charlie George. In defence there were veteran international defenders Dave Watson and Chris Nicholl.

The Dell was a quaint old English ground in those days, before the Taylor Report and all-seaters and before Saints needed to move to a new location to bring in more revenue. With a capacity then of 23,000 – which was eventually lowered to 15,000 prior to the club's move to St Mary's Stadium – the Dell had the most curious upper tier of terracing in one corner and its tight confines were always packed. Nowhere more so than the press box when Keegan came to town, so worthwhile to cover were the matches.

'What Lawrie did was stunning,' says Bob Harris. 'What the team did was phenomenal. They were great to watch, a smashing side. And it was always fun. You went to Southampton and you came away with a smile on your face.'

With Keegan to gild the lily, they could beat anybody at home – and did with Arsenal and Manchester United, doing the double over then powerful Leeds. They also drew with United at Old Trafford and Spurs (the score no fewer than four each) at White Hart Lane. Then again, they beat Watford 4–0 in the first leg of a League Cup tie only to lose the return 7–1.

For a while, Keegan revelled in these flamboyant days. 'I think Kevin would say he enjoyed his times with us because of the way we played,' says McMenemy. 'We had Micky and Steve Moran up front with him, Channon one side, Keegan the other, with Alan Ball behind and Dave Armstrong and Steve Williams there too. It was the perfect blend.

'He was top dog, king pin, but never asked for any favours and was totally respected by all the professionals in the game. He never missed training, though he might get a helicopter somewhere at the end of it. He was very popular with the media and advertising.

'I accepted that he was different but he didn't expect any different treatment. There's levels. You don't need to tell a superstar he's a superstar. People have an air about them, they seem ten feet tall. Kevin had that. He was captain of England, he had been around the world, he was confident in his own ability.'

Keegan loved the area and the company. 'Mick, Alan and Kevin were great pals and I had wonderful times with them,' adds McMenemy. 'You can either live with those players or you can't. I was able to.'

The football began to pall, however. Southampton finished sixth in his first season but he was not as impressed as everyone else, possibly because it had taken him until Christmas to find his goal-scoring touch. The place did not have the same passion for the game as Liverpool, nor the copious support or expectation on which he had thrived when he was last in England.

Now thirty, he had also suffered his first serious injury, a hamstring tear, and had consequently missed fifteen games. His mood towards the club was not best improved when he was pressed into service while still troubled by the injury, for reasons of public-relations on a trip to Casablanca.

He got over it for a while, though, and enjoyed a successful second season, scoring a remarkable thirty goals, twenty-six of which were in the League – with seven from the penalty spot – and winning the Golden Boot. There were some more astonishing results, too, including a 4–3 win over Ipswich and a 5–5 draw at home to Coventry. There were also 4–2 defeats at West Ham and Coventry.

They led the table at the end of January for the only time in their history, after wins over Liverpool, Leeds, Manchester United and Arsenal in the first half of the season and a 1–0 win at Middlesbrough courtesy of Keegan's goal. For a while it almost looked as if little old Southampton could even win the title. Keegan himself reckoned they needed reinforcements. He has since said that on the coach back from an away game he urged McMenemy to sign Peter Shilton to stop the leaking of goals – with Shilton on board they might just do it. According to Keegan's version of events, McMenemy asked him if he could help raise some finance for the deal.

McMenemy recalls it differently. 'I would never let a player tell me who to sign,' he says. 'Kevin had his opinion and I would listen if he said, "So and so is good", but I was strong-minded. I had proved myself. I never told anyone who I was signing.'

McMenemy was unable to sign new players to give the club a boost for the run-in and Keegan gradually grew disillusioned. Southampton won only three of their last fourteen games, which meant a seventh-place finish.

The relationship ended in some acrimony, with McMenemy and Keegan falling out over different versions of events. Keegan would say in his autobiography that he resented McMenemy calling the team, including him, cheats on one occasion after a poor performance. In view of later episodes in Keegan's career, there was also considerable irony in Keegan urging the manager to sign a goalkeeper because the team was conceding too many and thus there being too often pressure on the forwards to score enough. Peter Shilton joined the club that summer, McMenemy having failed to prise Ray Clemence out of Liverpool at the end of his career, just as it was all coming to a head.

By then, and by his own account, Keegan had had enough. He turned up for a pre-season tour to Ireland to see only youngsters, rather than the new players he claimed McMenemy had promised him he would be signing. The manager was absent, too, from the airport.

Keegan sensed that the good times had gone. He decided he wanted to be released to find a new club, which caused considerable anger within the city among fans who had already bought season tickets on the back of Keegan staying for another year. His lack of appetite suddenly for another season at the Dell may also have had a lot to do with Mick Channon leaving the club that summer.

'Kevin possibly hoped the club would match his ambitions but now, because of the clubs he's been at and the money he's had, he probably accepts more the fact of how well we did. We had finished top six; Kevin probably realised that that was going to be our limit and that he was still good enough to be playing at a top club.

'As a manager, I was looking to move on and I thought Mick Channon's legs had gone and I needed younger legs in. All of those factors made Kevin decide to go. He was a strong-minded, single-minded character and his mind was made up.

We tried everything we could, I even said, "Represent us in Europe."

'I wasn't happy. I was disappointed with him because I was losing my best player. We had a lot of problems because of the season tickets and to be fair he said, "Well, if it's a financial problem, I will pay." I said, "You have another year," and he said, "Well, I'll pack in then." In the end, you just had to shake hands and be grateful you had had him for two years.'

A coolness did develop between the two men for a while. 'We had a period when I didn't see him,' says McMenemy. 'But over the years we have kept in touch, the wives in particular.

'In his book he talked about that pre-season trip to Ireland, saying that I didn't turn up. I never, ever missed a trip and I got there the day after they did. I had been on a family holiday that was late because I was on the World Cup panel with the BBC. When I read that, I phoned him and bet him a bottle of Champagne I was on that trip. I won that bet.'

Mention of that World Cup of 1982 brings up something else that was badly affecting Keegan at the time. It concerned grief and a sense of grievance at the anticlimax of a World Cup that summer that had seen ruined what he'd hoped was going to be the crowning glory of his career: the England side he was due and desperate to captain becoming real contenders to the title of World Champions.

5

Country Man

How we pine for those days of the 1970s when the England manager had so many players to choose from, when there seemed to be such a glut of talent. How could they not succeed with goalkeepers like Peter Shilton and Ray Clemence, defenders such as Bobby Moore, Roy McFarland and Colin Todd, with Colin Bell in midfield and strikers such as Malcolm Macdonald and Allan Clarke? Then later in the decade Trevor Brooking, Steve Coppell and Trevor Francis? And this was without all those talented mavericks of the period like Tony Currie, Stan Bowles, Alan Hudson, Frank Worthington and Rodney Marsh.

Despite the apparent plethora of qualified and quality players, as opposed to these days when just over a third in the Premier League are eligible for England, how easily we can forget, too, just how poor was the national team's record in the most fallow of decades for them and us as they failed to qualify for the finals of a tournament between the World Cup quarter-final defeat to West Germany in Mexico, 1970 and the European Championships in Italy in 1980, though they did reach the last eight of that competition in 1972 only to be humbled over two legs, home and away, by the Germans, led by Gunter Netzer, whom Kevin Keegan would come to know at Hamburg.

It was Keegan's misfortune, at least for his place in the pantheon of England greats, that the peak years of his career coincided with those worst of times. Then again, there was an element of fortune for his personal profile that he emerged in the English game at a time of transition, when there was the chance for a young player to establish himself as a great old guard of 1966 World Cup winner, from Gordon Banks through the Charlton brothers to Geoff Hurst, was departing the scene.

Keegan's rise, too, came at a time when the domestic game may have seemed more authentic and gutsy compared to the sanitised, over-commercial experience of modern all-seater stadia but the reality was often dirty, dangerous grounds and dirty, dangerous football before the law modifications of the 1990s that outlawed the tackle from behind and returned the emphasis to attacking play. It was a decade when a workmanlike, brave and honest player could become a superstar.

Keegan made his debut against Wales in a World Cup qualifier in Cardiff in November 1972, six months after that European Championship defeat by West Germany, as Sir Alf Ramsey's side was falling into decline, by now having established himself just over a year into his Liverpool career. England won 1–0 but were not impressive. Of the debutant,

England, The Complete Post-War Record noted: 'When, in the last seconds, Ball put Kevin Keegan through, it seemed that the Liverpool star would celebrate his debut with a goal. Unfortunately, though, Keegan made a mess of trying to dribble around Sprake and the chance was lost.'

When England were booed off the Wembley pitch in the February return, in which John Toshack scored the Welsh goal in a 1–1 draw, Keegan became one of the victims of Ramsey's selection for a qualifying match in Poland, which England lost 2–0 to reveal creaks in the team, notably with Bobby Moore beginning to wane. Indeed, Keegan would never appear again under Ramsey in the next ten internationals, despite his growing contribution for Liverpool.

Ramsey seemed to have a mistrust of Keegan as a younger, flashier talent, preferring to stick with his tried and trusted lieutenants, as far as they were still around, that was. The manager was also at odds with the superstar cult that was developing, with the commercial world that was increasingly impinging on football and which Keegan, his hair long and sporting the Harold Steptoe sideburns in vogue at the time, was by now increasingly embracing.

The press was also growing more influential and vociferous, calling for Keegan to be in the side, but the more they did, the more the recalcitrant Ramsey dug in his heels.

It was a time of great change with which Ramsey was uncomfortable. Rupert Murdoch had bought the *Sun* newspaper in 1969, turned it tabloid and introduced the topless page three girl the following year. Under its innovative sports editor Frank Nicklin, seeing sport as a circulation-booster, it altered the way the game was covered, with quotes from players and managers used more extensively, with colourful, even brash, characters like Brian Clough and Malcolm Allison (of Manchester City then Crystal Palace) – both quite unlike the restrained Ramsey – only too happy to supply them. George Best and Jimmy Greaves started supplying outspoken ghost-written columns.

On that fateful autumn night of 1973 in the Wembley return against the Poles, which became one of those 'where-were-you-when?' nights for a generation, Keegan sat agitatedly on the bench as a substitute, Bobby Moore – dropped after that debacle in the away game in Katowice – among those also sitting it out.

They saw a tense game, goalless at half-time, when ITV pundit Clough urged the nation to relax, make a cup of tea, put its feet up and enjoy England scoring second-half goals against the clown Jan Tomaszewski in goal. Then Norman Hunter allowed Grzegorz Lato to escape him and feed Jan Domarski for a shot that slithered under Shilton's body. England, unbelievably, were a goal behind. But wait. Allan Clarke scored an equaliser from the penalty spot and England launched a barrage at the Polish goal.

Keegan thought he was going to get on to the field at that point. Substitutes were a relatively new phenomenon, having been introduced only in 1965 for injured players then allowed also for tactical reasons in 1967. Ramsey was not best practised in using them, rarely used them, indeed, even in friendlies. Quite probably he was bruised by that experience in Mexico in 1970 when England led their World Cup quarter-final against West Germany 2–0 but lost 3–2 and Ramsey brought off Bobby Charlton and Martin Peters as the mayhem was unfolding.

But with Moore at his side urging him to change things now, Ramsey finally two minutes from time shouted down the bench for 'Kevin' to get changed. Keegan's ears pricked up but it turned out to be Kevin Hector, the Derby County striker, that Ramsey was calling on for a debut. He came close but could not score – Hector's only two appearances for England would last twenty-one minutes – and England had failed to reach the 1974 finals in West Germany.

After an initial numbness, the rest was hysteria. Ramsey, '66 World Cup winner and '70 quarter-finalist, clung on for a while – which would be remarkable these days but Ramsey had earned some respect and the climate of the times was not for sacking – but the following spring, and a couple of matches later, he was gone.

The absorbent Keegan, always noting what was happening around him due to his thirst for life and the game, as well as gleaning experience for the future, would later say diplomatically in his autobiography that he had been fond of Ramsey, admiring him for being unafraid both to give Keegan his debut and also to drop him. He considered him a 'players' man', too much of one even, Ramsey being fortunate to operate at a time when the media, with whom he had an offhand relationship, was less pervasive and intrusive, though that was inexorably turning at around that time.

Actually, elsewhere Keegan would let slip his real resentment about his treatment under Ramsey. 'I do not think Alf rated me as a player,' Dave Bowler, in his biography of Sir Alf, *Winning Isn't Everything,* quoted him as saying. 'Pressure from outside influenced his decision to call me into the squad and select me for the team . . . Usually he picked players who he believed were capable of doing a job for him. How else could a player like Peter Storey have won so many caps? No doubt Sir Alf would disagree but other people wanted me to play and he had reached a situation where he had to try something new.'

It was the end of an era and as he had proved so often in penalty areas, Keegan was the right man in the right place at the right time. With so many experienced players departing, Keegan was immediately returned to the team by the caretaker manager Joe Mercer for the end-of-season Home Internationals and a tour of Eastern Europe. Keegan's autobiography recalls him being captain for that trip but it was in fact his Liverpool colleague Emlyn Hughes. He would have to wait another two years for that honour.

Fresh from having scored twice against Newcastle to win the FA Cup with Liverpool, the game against Wales – Keegan's third cap coming like the first two against the country where he now lived, in the countryside south of Liverpool – also saw his first goal for his country as England won 2–0. They beat Northern Ireland but lost 2–0 to Scotland, just ahead of their appearance in the World Cup finals, with Keegan rested ahead of a friendly against Argentina at Wembley, which would be drawn.

Keegan quickly took to Mercer, the former Manchester City manager but now a director of Coventry City, on the tour that took in games against East Germany in Leipzig, Bulgaria in Sofia and Yugoslavia in Belgrade. Mercer, a genial, avuncular character, had a bad back and was unable to take the training but created a conducive mood to which Keegan responded and which left a lasting impression.

Looking back, Keegan credits Mercer with much of his own philosophy that he took into management, indeed, and with the benefit of hindsight, his analysis is telling.

'Joe just told us to go out and enjoy ourselves,' Keegan said. 'It was a game of pleasure, he would say. I probably carried into my management career more of Joe Mercer than of any other manager I knew, including Bill Shankly.

'I tried to do with my sides what Joe did with his. He wanted to be remembered for things like flair and flamboyance, the sort of characteristics they tell you cannot win titles . . . I could relate to him and his ethos. He proved that his style of football could work at the highest level.'

England drew 1–1 in Leipzig then won 1–0 in Sofia before a bizarre and violent episode at Belgrade airport involving

Keegan. As international incidents go, it may not have been in quite the same league as Bobby Moore and the allegedly pilfered Bogota bracelet before the 1970 World Cup but it certainly created plenty of diplomatic waves.

It was witnessed by Bob Harris, then chief sports writer of Thomson Regional Newspapers, which served thirty daily and evening provincial papers around the country, before he went on to become sports editor of the *Sunday Mirror*.

Harris, who covered all of Keegan's sixty-three appearances for England, would often play cribbage with Keegan and Trevor Brooking – how innocent it all sounds now in the era of England players amusing themselves with Playstations, I-Pods and Wiis – along with the *Daily Mirror* photographer Monte Fresco, a Cockney who is credited with coining the nickname for Keegan which stuck amongst his teammates, too. 'Andy' came from the Andy Capp strip in the *Daily Mirror* because, Harris explains, 'he was a little Northern fellow'.

'Kevin wasn't one of the wild boys at all, but one of the few times that Kevin had a late night was on that tour,' Harris recalls. 'I think he was a bit hungover, if not tired, when we straggled through customs. We were all mixed together, journalists and players, with Uncle Joe at the back. They weren't in uniform, which was a big mistake, but it was a relaxed tour and very hot.

'Five or six of us were through and Andy sat on the baggage carousel, which wasn't going round at the time because no bags had come off yet. He was very tired. All of a sudden some guards were on the scene and instead of asking him to stand up and get off, they dragged him off. He was cross, as was everyone else there. The moment he opened his mouth they were all over him and dragged him to an office and beat the little bugger. Literally beat him.'

Harris dashed off to find Mercer and the Football Association secretary Ted Croker. 'By then it was a question of saving face,' says Harris. 'The Yugoslavs were saying that he had misbehaved, which he hadn't, and the FA were demanding he was released.

'Joe had been very quiet on this tour, it was the end of his career and everyone adored him. He would always say, "Come and have a word, tell me about the opposition so I know what I am talking about." He was as good as gold.

'But when it came to this moment, he was as strong as anyone around. He insisted that Keegan was released, and they had to. Mercer said that nobody was leaving the room until they released him. They wanted to hold on to his passport but Mercer said that if it wasn't returned, England wouldn't play Yugoslavia. It became massive.

'The next thing, little Andy was playing, insisted he played in fact, and his strength impressed me, because it took a lot out of him that did.' Keegan grabbed the equaliser in a 2–2 draw with a brave diving header and emerged with the whole incident having enhanced him. His goal was a thank-you to Mercer – who thus ended his stewardship with a record of played seven, won three, drawn three and lost one – for the new impetus to his international career.

Keegan still worried about who might be the new England manager, however. There was a clamour for Clough, but his public criticisms of the FA were hard for the blazers of the international committee to forgive or forget. Malcolm Allison had his admirers but his showbiz populism at the time – though he would prove a brilliant club coach – was too tacky for the decision-makers. When it was announced that it would be Don Revie, Keegan was initially suspicious, but then most of the country was.

Revie had built a successful but unpopular side at Leeds United, who had just won their second League title under him. They were noted for ruthlessness and questionable sportsmanship, even if most grudgingly accepted that those such as Johnny Giles and Billy Bremner could play a bit too. Liverpool had a fierce rivalry with Leeds, physically and emotionally, in that era and on Merseyside, Keegan was part of the distaste for the methods in West Yorkshire.

But Keegan took to his fellow Yorkshireman, Revie's birthplace of Middlesbrough then still deemed a part of the county. The start was hugely encouraging, a 3–0 win over Czechoslovakia at Wembley, and Keegan admired the sense of patriotism that Revie instilled, with the singing of 'Land of Hope and Glory' being reintroduced before Wembley internationals. He even entered into the spirit of the bingo and carpet putting that the manager employed for bonding and harmony but which some players ridiculed. Keegan, though – in another insight into how he would himself manage – did not agree with Revie's obsessive dossiers on the opposition, believing the game to be more about how you played.

Keegan also gave credit to Revie for saving him from himself on one occasion. With the Troubles in full cry in Belfast, the FA received a death threat against Keegan ahead of the 1975 match against Northern Ireland in the Home International tournament – England's first visit to the province in five years – but Keegan insisted on playing. By his own admission, his performance was limited as, understandably worried, he confined himself to central areas of the pitch.

When he was subsequently omitted for the game against Wales the following midweek, he took it as a snub and left the team hotel in a fit of the knee-jerk pique and emotionalism with which he would later become associated. Revie telephoned Keegan's home and explained that he wanted to save him for the following game against Scotland and Keegan, by now having cooled down after the long journey home, agreed to return to the squad. It also said something about Revie's management at the time. Frequently criticised for making too many changes, the manager's problem was also that he sometimes omitted to inform the players of his decisions, thus alienating them and stoking a discontent that would make the papers.

'He talked him back but Revie was also bright and knew that Kevin wasn't the man in the squad he should just let walk away,' says Bob Harris. 'Revie was one of the shrewdest people I ever met in my life. He could also be devious. But Don was remarkable too. He knew how to manipulate people, which was something Kevin couldn't do, and he also knew how to motivate them, which Kevin could also do.'

Keegan emerged as Revie's first-choice striker, not surprisingly given his consistent form for Liverpool and his growing stature in the English game. He even gave him the captaincy for the first time against Wales in Wrexham in 1976, the season in which Liverpool would win the European Cup-Winners' Cup against Bruges and Keegan become the Footballer of the Year voted by the country's journalists. Indeed later that year, with Revie's first-choice captain Gerry Francis so often injured, Revie would make Keegan his full-time skipper.

If there was a love affair between the two, it was not shared by the rest of the country. After that promising start against Czechoslovakia, England lost the return in Bratislava and it would be the Czechs who qualified for the latter stages of the 1976 European Championship.

Worse was to follow when England failed to reach the finals of the 1978 World Cup in Argentina, the damage done by a failure to score enough goals in their qualifying group against Finland and Luxembourg, with Italy going through having beaten England 2–0 in Rome but losing by 2–0 at Wembley.

An insecure man despite his achievements, Revie feared the sack as the campaign neared its conclusion. He was fearful, too, of financial insecurity, having seen his hero when a lad watching Middlesbrough, Wilf Mannion, end up as a tea boy in a local factory. Clandestinely, Revie negotiated a then lucrative contract of £60,000 a year tax free to manage in the United Arab Emirates to where he decamped after England's summer tour to South America in 1977, on which Keegan was captain, fresh from Liverpool's European Cup triumph and prior to beginning pre-season with Hamburg.

Condemnation was widespread, Revie having sullied the position deemed so honourable under Ramsey. It seemed appropriate that the whole tawdry reign was associated with a new England strip, produced by a company called Admiral, departing from the traditional white with a new design that incorporated red and blue patches and flashes. Now, to fans sadly and mostly used to changes, it would be nothing untoward. Then it was seen as tacky.

The FA chairman Sir Harold Thompson was incandescent, perhaps because Revie jumped before he could push him, perhaps because he read about it first in the *Daily Mail*, which had paid Revie £20,000 for the exclusive. The organisation charged Revie with bringing the game into disrepute. The ten-year ban they imposed was overturned in the High Court, however.

Soon allegations emerged to damage Revie even further of an alleged attempt to bribe a Wolverhampton Wanderers player in a decisive League match against Leeds in 1972. Said Alan Hardaker, the Football League's autocratic secretary, of the Revie departure: 'Don Revie's decision doesn't surprise me in the slightest. Now I only hope he can quickly learn how to call out bingo numbers in Arabic.'

Keegan, always industrious and one of the few redeeming elements amid their struggles through the failures to reach major finals, remained untainted by the Revie controversy and would continue as England's talisman for another half a decade as the upright Ron Greenwood of West Ham was appointed, first as caretaker then full-time, with the FA ignoring more public and press support for Clough, with Lawrie McMenemy and Bobby Robson now also in the frame.

Not that being turned down at what was still an early stage of his managerial career turned off the then Ipswich manager Robson from attending England games and purring over Keegan.

'Because I played for my country, I used to love going to Wembley to see the internationals and I never missed one,' he recalls. 'If we had a player in the team, like Micky Mills or Paul Mariner, as a manager you would get two tickets. I used to love it.

'I used to come back and say to my players, "Last night I saw the bravest, littlest, most courageous and effervescent player I will ever see in my life. I wish you all could have been there to see it." He was a little dynamo. He went into the box, went in on headers, went on dribbles and was looking to get on the end of a through pass even though he knew there would be a tackle.

'I remember England playing Scotland [a 3–1 win at Wembley in 1979] and he played a one-two with Trevor Brooking. He got on this ball as two defenders were converging on it and you thought he might pull out but he got between them just as they crashed into him but still beat the goalkeeper. That was the crucial goal and England went on to win comfortably.

'He was a great role model for young players. He had a lot of qualities, was a great little finisher. He was probably the highest-paid English player at that time but there was a reason for that – because he gave more than anyone else.'

At least under Greenwood, dignified and understated, if sometimes prickly with the press, England qualified again for tournaments. They were fortunate in the qualifying draw for the 1980 European Championships and breezed through a group that included Northern Ireland, the Republic of Ireland, Denmark and Bulgaria. It helped, too, that the tournament would feature eight teams in the finals, rather than four, for the first time.

England indeed won seven and drew the other of their eight games but flopped when it came to the finals in Italy. Having tried several captains, Greenwood had returned to Keegan and optimism was high.

However, after seeing their side take the lead against Belgium in Turin, only to concede an equaliser, a section of England's fans grew angry and aggressive, and were subjected to tear gas from the Italian police. England then lost 1–0 to the host nation and despite a 2–1 win over Spain were eliminated at the group stage, Belgium having drawn with Italy.

Now twenty-nine, and at Southampton, qualifying for the '82 World Cup in Spain became hugely significant for Keegan. All began well, with three wins, but come the May of 1981, England were beaten 2–1 by Switzerland in Basle and fans went on the rampage. All hell broke loose back home, too, but England recovered the situation with an unlikely 3–1 win in Hungary, Keegan scoring from the penalty spot and Brooking scoring twice, in one of the goals the ball memorably becoming lodged in a stanchion.

From a stronger position after the victory, Greenwood now contemplated quitting and spoke to his captain privately about it. On the flight home, however, the senior players Keegan, Brooking, Ray Clemence and Mick Mills talked him out of it.

'If that was player power, it was player power in its best sense,' Keegan would come to reflect. 'As a manager you feel very isolated and even leaders need encouragement sometimes. They occasionally need to be told "well done" just as the foot soldiers do. When I was in charge at Newcastle, Peter Beardsley supported me in this way for a while and most of the other players did so after I had left – that was nice, but it was too late then.'

Still there was drama before qualifying was secured, with England losing 2–1 to Norway to prompt the celebrated commentary by a local television man that informed 'birthplace of giants' England – including Lord Nelson, Lord Beaverbook, Sir Winston Churchill, Sir Anthony Eden, Clement Attlee, Henry Cooper, Lady Diana and Maggie Thatcher – that 'your boys took a hell of a beating'. Finally the heartache ended when England beat group winners Hungary 1–0 at Wembley and qualified.

Keegan, along with Brooking, having helped to persuade Greenwood to remain in the job in the midst of crisis may be a reason why the manager was so indulgent towards the pair, who were by now the creative hub of England and gelled so well together, when it came to the World Cup finals of 1982 in Spain, in what was to be one of the greatest disappointments of Keegan's career.

He may well have worried during the winter when the Falklands conflict was playing itself out, and there were suggestions that England should not compete when they might meet Argentina, but the concern eased with the British retaking the islands and the World Cup draw keeping the two nations apart.

And so with Bryan Robson having emerged, England entered the tournament feeling they had a real chance, the more so as Argentina, Brazil and Italy were in a section of the draw where they could destroy each other. 'We all thought we could win it,' says Bob Harris. 'The players believed we had the team to win that, Ron Greenwood believed it.'

Keegan, now thirty-one, had waited close to a decade to perform on the biggest of stages but now he inflamed an old back injury just a week before the tournament. Brooking had developed a groin strain, too, and England suddenly seemed in a sorry state, shorn of their captain, their two best players indeed. Keegan's injury became the main talking point.

At first none worried too much, as England beat France 3–1 then Czechoslovakia 2–0 to make sure of a place in the second phase even before their third group match. Still unfit, Keegan saw his World Cup disappearing, though, and grew restless and discontented around England's base camp near Bilbao. He and Brooking were almost apart from the squad but were having an effect on it. At least Keegan was.

'He was at his worst and it did a lot of damage,' Harris recalls. 'He was crabby, as you would be, and it spread around the squad.' Only news from home that Keegan had been awarded the OBE lifted his spirits.

'Kevin and Trevor roomed together and were together all the time, jogged around the pitch together,' Harris continues. 'Trevor was almost cast in the same light but he was never a problem. He is a different character to Kevin, who wears everything on his sleeve, good or bad. He is easily upset and it shows throughout his career and his life.' Greenwood, indeed, even went to speak to Keegan one day to ask him to improve his downbeat demeanour.

Keegan had two years since completed his time with Hamburg but wanted to travel to Germany to see a specialist he trusted. Greenwood was sceptical. He agreed only after an epidural from the England team doctor which did not work. By now, Keegan was even more desperate. England had beaten Kuwait 1–0 in their final group game and were preparing for the second phase, which at that tournament was a three-team group that included the host nation Spain and Keegan's old host nation, West Germany.

According to Keegan, Greenwood wanted the trip to see the German specialist kept quiet. And so began an extraordinary sequence of secret events that just could not happen in modern times. Keegan borrowed a tiny Seat 500 car from a hotel employee to drive himself overnight to Madrid from Bilbao for a dawn flight to Hamburg. Then, after treatment, he was back in the camp within forty-eight hours, having also driven back from Madrid to Bilbao in the Seat.

'He went off like a thief in the night,' says Harris. 'It wouldn't be allowed now. However good the treatment, the driving made the back worse, something we all wrote when we found out.'

To his great disappointment, Keegan missed the goalless draw with West Germany, featuring his old Hamburg teammate Manny Kaltz, who were not at their strongest and were there for the taking. Now, to reach the semi-finals, England had to beat Spain, who had lost to the Germans in the group's other game, by two clear goals. Greenwood's dilemma was whether to stick with the side that had brought England to this point or restore the undoubtedly influential Keegan and Brooking.

Greenwood consulted his faithful and capable assistant Don Howe, whom Keegan always had reservations about due to his reputation as a defensive coach and because he had once, according to Keegan, called Brooking a 'cheat' in a team meeting due to his fitful tracking back to defend, a word the players forced Howe to retract.

After weighing it all up, in what Keegan would, with regret and even anger, call 'Ron Greenwood's biggest mistake', he made them substitutes but as the clock ticked down with the game goalless, both would get their chance. And both, famously, would get chances. On they came with twenty-six minutes to go. Brooking burst through but saw a low shot saved brilliantly by Luis Arconada in the Spanish goal. He then fashioned a cross from which Keegan, just half a dozen yards out, seemed certain to add to his twenty-one goals for his country. The ball was screwed wide off those curls, however, and the game petered out to a goalless draw.

Their sharpness had not returned, could not in such a short time. 'How do you expect anything of players who haven't played for a month?' Harris wonders. England were out, without losing a game.

All were crestfallen, knowing that a marvellous opportunity to reach the semi-finals had been spurned, the more so when from another group the French would make the last four despite having been beaten by England in their opening game.

Keegan took it especially hard. He may still have harboured thoughts of another World Cup despite the fact that he would then be in his mid-thirties but he must have sensed deep down that his peak was past. He could not have known, though, that the truncated cameo against Spain would prove, controversially, his last game for England, the header wide his last meaningful action for his country.

Bobby Robson was to succeed the resigning Greenwood and made a first decision that stunned the nation, no one more than Keegan. When the new manager announced his first squad, for a European Championship qualifier against Denmark in Copenhagen in September 1982, there was no place for Keegan.

'It was always my feeling that it was down to conversations with Don Howe and possibly Ron,' says Bob Harris. 'If Ron told him the story of the World Cup, then you go, "I do not need that in my squad."

'Bobby knew Kevin had a big influence on the players around him and thought, rightly or wrongly, this is my team, I have just taken over and I'm not going to start with Kevin Keegan.'

Keegan hit the roof, went to the press to say that the least he had deserved was a phone call from Robson. Now having left Southampton amid some controversy after his World Cup disappointment to take up a new challenge with then Second Division Newcastle United as a player, Keegan claimed that Robson had even said to him, 'See you in a couple of weeks,' when he came to see his first game at St James' Park that August, against Queen's Park Rangers, in which Keegan scored the only goal.

'He may be right but I can't remember it,' says Robson, who would get a cool reception from some Newcastle fans for some years as a result of his rift with Keegan, despite being one of their own. 'I went to the game with my father and I don't remember talking to Kevin afterwards.

'I had a difficult decision. The fact that he had gone out of the First Division into the Second worried me. He hadn't had a good World Cup trip and I just thought, "Is he kind of saying I am finished with international football?" So I left him out of the side and there were a few recriminations when I announced my first squad.

'He felt I should have rung him and maybe I should on reflection. But I didn't owe him that because I didn't know him, had never spoken to him. I had never been his manager. I was the England manager, I had a squad to put out and I wanted to say, "That's my squad, no explanations, that's it."

'I remember thinking, do I start afresh – new squad, new beginning? There were others, like Brooking. I never chose Brooking again, but I admired him a great deal.

'That's the way I felt. I thought about whether I should

discard those who were not going to be long term and I thought I would go with the young element but I will go back to him if I need to.

'What I should have done, should have said, is "Kevin, I am leaving you out of the team, I am going to start with a new squad, but what I want to know from you is that if the players I bring in are not good enough and don't rise to the occasion, would you be prepared to come back?" Maybe I should have handled it that way but I didn't.

'I never brought him back in the end. But I had Peter Beardsley, Chris Waddle, John Barnes, Luther Blissett and Gary Lineker came soon. There were forwards in the country at the time.

'I have made my peace with him. I saw him once or twice after that and we are grown-up. We both know what the game brings, some animosity sometimes, not unfriendliness, but I made peace with him and got along fine. I did what I felt I had to do. I didn't bear any grudges and he didn't seem to either. We just got on with life.'

Keegan's life by now had taken a new turn, was heading in a different direction. For, brushing aside his World Cup gloom, he was beginning a love affair with that club he had believed from childhood he was destined to represent.

6

Goals to Newcastle

Even if memories of conversations with Kevin Keegan elude him, Bobby Robson remembers well the mood that day. 'He was the idol. The place was crammed and he played quite well, actually. They were all just waiting for him to score a goal and I thought the heavens would open. Sure enough, that's what he did. He scored a goal. The whole stadium was alight. He was mobbed.'

It was 28 August 1982, barely a couple of months after that World Cup agony, barely a couple of weeks after Keegan had decided that he had had enough of Southampton. He had contacted his agent, Harry Swales, about finding him a new club; Swales had already spoken casually to Newcastle's Arthur Cox and Stan Seymour, manager and chairman respectively, and knew they were interested.

Was Keegan tapped up? None of the recorded versions of the move by the various parties involved ever mentions such a thing but the game is a gossipy, villagey world and the line between illegal approaches and hypothetical conversations was as thin then as it is now whenever managers, players, agents and now chief executives shoot the breeze.

Lawrie McMenemy knew of the admiration Arthur Cox – gruff but engaging old-style football manager – had for Keegan, having received that phone call when he pulled off the coup of signing the player from Hamburg. So Keegan would have been aware of it too. And if his agent knew that Newcastle wanted him, so did Keegan.

Keegan had been put off staying on the South Coast not only by the prospect of another season spent clinging to the coat-tails of the bigger clubs, rather than competing intensely with them, and of Southampton not being able to afford the players he would have liked them to sign. He also recognised that his career needed excitement, new footballing stimulation and impetus after that gloomy World Cup experience.

Cox insisted that all was above board. 'At the end of my first year I arranged to have a meal with Harry Swales,' he says. 'After the meal I told Harry, "Look, I've got the best supporters in the country and a massive club. I want a player to do for us what Dave Mackay did for Derby County. I want Kevin Keegan to come to Newcastle – but only when the time is right. And if this gets out on to the street, forget it. I don't want anything improper going on. You call me when you are ready."'

Swales did call, that August, and Keegan found himself meeting at a hotel in London with Cox, Seymour, the Newcastle secretary, Russell Cushing, and Alistair Wilson of Scottish and

Newcastle Breweries – sponsors of the club, who were going to be helping with financing the deal.

'Nobody leaves here until you sign for Newcastle United,' said Cox. Keegan, who had also spoken to Manchester United, then managed in the pre-Alex Ferguson era by Ron Atkinson, replied that he wanted this done quickly. A horse in which he had a stake was running that afternoon. As with McMenemy, the talks did not take long, since Keegan had already made up his mind. He wanted to go 'home'.

With time running out on his playing career, he could see a golden chance to finally join the club of his father's fables. Dad Joe had died some six years earlier, but Keegan knew he would have been proud. And how many sons the world over want to please their fathers or honour their memory?

A golden chance and a silver lining, too, to Keegan's pockets. Newcastle were at the time a mid-table Second Division club – they'd languished there for four years at this point – but they could afford him because at Southampton he shrewdly insisted, once again, that his contract contained a maximum transfer fee, this time of £100,000. It left him free to negotiate favourable terms.

Keegan had learnt enough about the commercial world and this knowledge, along with his sharply developed sense of his own worth and the drive of the working man who recalls his humble roots, enabled him to negotiate quite a contract.

It was a time when English football was still blighted by hooliganism; the game, though enduringly popular, had not yet become as central to English culture in the way inspired by the formation of the Premier League a decade later, with the marketing, merchandising and above all copious television coverage that came with it. Before the mid-eighties disasters of Heysel, Bradford and Hillsborough, stadiums were still basic, particularly on the terraces, and the prevailing feeling was that live TV would detract from attendances rather than enhance them.

Tyneside has never needed much excuse to overdose on optimism when it comes to Newcastle United and when Keegan conducted another of his masterly press conferences the city was suitably excited – even if the football world was not quite as stunned as it was the day he signed for Southampton. The Newcastle secretary, Russell Cushing, eschewing his reputation for understatement, announced: 'We're in heaven – we've got Kevin.'

'No other player in the world could have had such a dramatic effect on the club and its supporters,' Arthur Cox would say.

The players themselves were delighted; even Mick Martin, the midfield player who would have to concede the captaincy to Keegan. 'It didn't bother me in the least,' he said. 'My attitude was that it didn't matter, if we got promotion.'

Said Chris Waddle – then a gangling kid who had just come from part-timers Tow Law Town and working in a sausage factory, long before he played for Spurs, Marseille and England – of that opening-day game against Queen's

Park Rangers: 'I was standing waiting to kick-off and I was in a daze. There was Kevin Keegan playing in the same team as me.'

There were 36,185 inside St James' Park that day, including a young teenager who played for Wallsend Boys Club named Alan Shearer. Though scarcely comparing with the attendances in the all-seater stadium now, it was still capacity and quite some attendance for a distinctly average team in the second tier. The more so when compared with Newcastle's last home gate of the previous season: fewer than 10,000 against Wrexham.

Keegan had negotiated for fifteen per cent of the gate receipts on anything above 15,000, since he and the club agreed that, should receipts increase, he was the man having the most effect. The idea came to him, he said, just as chairman Seymour was talking in the negotiations about just what effect Keegan would have on the club. It was clever stuff. Not only did it reveal Keegan's ability to think on his feet but also forced the chairman to reach a deal to back up his words.

It was also the forerunner to many later complicated transactions. These days it's commonplace for contracts to contain myriad clauses about crowd bonuses and image rights, the player's percentage of shirt and merchandise sales in his name. Keegan was furthering his reputation for inventive and imaginative financial arrangements with the game still backward in business terms. Many players in the future would have reason to be grateful.

Such were the crowds that season (averaging more than 24,000) and such were the bonuses (exact sums were never disclosed, to avoid upsetting other players) that Keegan later confessed to being embarrassed by them. He even claimed to have surrendered other bonuses owed to him, because he was doing so well. Among his bonuses was a deal with the local Scottish and Newcastle Breweries to coach kids and attend fans' forums in their pubs and clubs in the area. The only drawback seemed to be that a young practical joker of an apprentice was assigned to clean his boots. His name was Paul Gascoigne.

The crowd bonus might even have been much higher had Newcastle kept up a promising start. The 1–0 win over QPR saw Keegan caught up in the moment, declaring the fans better than Liverpool's and this the proudest day of his life (perhaps another reason why some of the Kop's feeling for him became diluted). Newcastle then won 2–1 at Blackburn; Keegan scored again but was not happy.

'We spent the entire second half camped in our own half lumping the ball forward,' Mick Martin recalled. 'Kevin came into the dressing-room at the end and said, "I can't be doing with that all season." He just wasn't used to it.'

Newcastle then went five games without a win before Cox – almost certainly with his captain's input – signed an old Anfield team-mate of Keegan's, Terry McDermott. The decline was duly arrested with a 5–1 win at Rotherham, in which Keegan scored four. The game was featured on *Match of the Day* and led to calls for him to be restored to the England side but Bobby Robson was not for turning.

It was a false dawn for an average side. Keegan asked Cox the whereabouts of all the promising young players that the manager had talked about when he signed. Beyond Waddle and McDermott, there was just not enough for promotion. Keegan may have been wondering if he, like the *Titanic*, should never have left Southampton.

Newcastle slumped as low as fifteenth when an eye injury sustained in a testimonial match just before Christmas forced Keegan to miss five games. He did form a potent partnership with the raw Imre Varadi, both scoring twenty-one League goals – six of Keegan's from the penalty spot – but ultimately Newcastle finishing fifth, three points short of promotion in those pre-playoff days, was a flattering position.

Keegan enjoyed working with Cox, whom he likened to Shankly for his passion and intensity about the game. A hard man with piercing eyes, Cox liked to concentrate on training and building the team; he was comfortable out of the limelight of press conferences, which he left to Keegan. It was something that meant the men would complement each other in the future, too.

Keegan had liked Cox's honesty when they first met. The manager had admitted that Newcastle were still a poor team, one that Keegan would improve immeasurably. These were sentiments that clearly appealed to and flattered Keegan. The club would, however, gradually acquire more and better players, Cox insisted. The resources would be in place. Keegan's Southampton experiences had made him wary, and now he was frustrated.

'I'm not holding a gun to their heads but I want to see some movement from the club,' he told the local press. 'I want to play with a better all-round squad next season so we gain more success. It's as much for the benefit of the fans as myself.'

Canny as ever. It would be the first time of many that the board of directors of Newcastle United were spurred into action by his words. It was the stuff about the fans that did it for them. Those fans were on Keegan's side and he knew it. The board would be the villains of the piece if they did not comply. Given assurances, Keegan signed for another year.

Cox sold Imre Varadi to Sheffield Wednesday, deeming his touch not good enough. Keegan, his standards high, may well have had some input into the decision: it was believed that he was not keen to play alongside Varadi. Six games into the season Cox now cleverly recruited a young lad who had been at Carlisle, then failed to make it at Manchester United before trying to kick-start his career with Vancouver Whitecaps in Canada. His name was Peter Beardsley.

At Christmas defender Glenn Roeder, from Queen's Park Rangers, also proved to be an inspired buy. With Waddle growing in confidence, having been somewhat overawed the previous season, a skilful combination of Keegan, Beardsley and Waddle suddenly gave Newcastle a cutting edge. 'I felt like the general in the trenches with the troops,' Keegan would say.

After Beardsley's arrival Newcastle assembled six consecutive wins. A 5–0 win over fellow promotion contenders Manchester City – Beardsley three, Keegan and Waddle one each – gave sensational notice that this could well be their season. That said, Tyneside was becoming used to dashed expectation, despite its propensity to optimism.

Something was to happen that January, however, midway through the season, that would certainly dent Kevin Keegan's optimism. Even alter the shape of his career and life.

All was going well enough. Newcastle were on course for promotion in the League and Keegan, McDermott and Newcastle had been sent to Liverpool for an evocative FA Cup third-round tie. Keegan was looking forward to returning to Anfield and receiving his dues from the crowd, though he knew that Liverpool – who were champions and would win the European Cup that season – were likely to give them a serious spanking.

They did. Liverpool won 4–0. What was unexpected to Keegan, and much more of a shock to his system, was an episode during the game.

Keegan knocked a ball past the leggy Liverpool defender Mark Lawrenson and set off after it, doing what he had done thousands of times before: asking himself what he was now going to do with the ball, checking in his mind's eye the position of the goalkeeper and the next defender, as all top players do. They will tell you they have a picture of the game in their head at any given time, can tell you who is located where.

This time, as never before, it was fanciful. Suddenly the swift Lawrenson had outpaced him to steal the ball. Keegan's thought process, the instinctive pattern of a great player, had been rudely interrupted. Though he didn't show it outwardly, and while few in the ground, if any, could have sensed how shocking was the moment to him, inwardly the stuffing was knocked from Keegan. He was crushed, his pride battered. For such a professional and fierce competitor, he had fallen short of his high standards, realised that he had lost something. His game had developed many facets down the years, ingenuity now accompanying the industry, but pace had always been a cornerstone and now it was overtaken by youth. Deep inside his competitor's being, he realised he could go on no longer.

At the end of the match, he shook hands with Lawrenson and the rest of the Liverpool team, accepted the applause of the Kop and returned to the dressing-room to tell Arthur Cox that he would see this season through, do his best to get Newcastle up into the First Division, and would then retire. Cox sensed that he meant it, as all who have known Keegan can tell when his mind really is made up, and did not argue strenuously. Perhaps he thought, as have others over the years, that Keegan might change his mind when the heat of the moment had passed.

I asked Lawrenson about the moment. 'When I finished him?' he joked. 'It didn't stick out, but I remember the day. We battered them.

'I remember that Terry McDermott was playing. People had seen him in Liverpool during the day in the hotel and said he had a cold sore on his lip. So one of the lads went to the joke shop and we all put cold sores on in the dressing-room. Then we got one of the backroom staff to go and tell him to come into the dressing-room and say hello. There we were with all these cold sores on.

'They also had Kevin, Chris Waddle, Peter Beardsley. And we smacked them four. I had known Arthur Cox since I was thirteen or fourteen. He was first-team coach at Preston and came for training after school twice a week on Tuesday and Thursday and used to kick me and kick me. I was a left-winger then. I used to think, "What on earth is this all about?" And then I kicked him back one day and he went, "I don't need to come any more. The penny's dropped."

'Anyway, I didn't realise that after the match Kevin has come into Arthur and said, "That's it." Later when I saw Kevin's quote about what had made him decide to pack in, I turned round and said that if I hadn't caught him I would have packed in myself. I would have been disappointed if I hadn't caught him.'

Five weeks later, on his thirty-third birthday, Keegan made his decision public. There was a lot of 'say it ain't so' reaction but he had determined on his course. And we were getting to know what that meant. Cox's instinct that arguing was pointless had proved accurate.

Keegan was as good as his word about his commitment for the rest of the season. Newcastle finished third, behind Chelsea and Sheffield Wednesday, to take the final promotion spot; he, Beardsley and Waddle had between them contributed sixty-five goals, with Keegan's own tally at twenty-seven. In all, in seventy-eight games for Newcastle, he scored forty-eight goals.

Keegan's final match for the club would go down in folklore and he would almost come to resent it. Liverpool came to St James' Park for a benefit game in which he put a penalty past Bruce Grobbelaar, and after which there was one last fanfare – a helicopter arriving to spirit him away. Proceeds from the game, Keegan pointed out, went not to him but to Newcastle for strengthening the side ahead of the following season.

Keegan's professional playing career was over. In all, he played 592 League games and scored 204 League goals. In two countries he had won five titles, three domestic cups and three European trophies.

Now he was tired, and tired of the game, too, it seemed. Not for him a quick entry into management. Indeed, he vowed for some time that he would never become a football manager. He had been involved in the intensity of the game, constantly training and playing, for sixteen years and wanted a complete break. He had also been in the media spotlight for much of that time and wanted respite. He took his wife Jean and the two daughters they now had, Laura and Sarah, to the warmth and good life of Marbella.

For the first year he travelled the world, playing a couple of games for an Australian side, Black Town, with Pele in an exhibition match in Tokyo, and coaching kids. He then settled down to a life mostly of golf and a little tennis. He got reacquainted with his old England manager, Don Revie, who was living on the Costa Del Sol, and became his golf partner. To Keegan's great sadness, Revie was then afflicted by and eventually killed by motor neurone disease.

There was after-dinner speaking, business ventures here and there, renovating and selling a house. He even came back to Newcastle once, to help Scottish and Newcastle Breweries fend off a takeover bid as a favour to his old friend Alistair Wilson.

Mostly, though, the obsession was his golf handicap, which he managed to get down to an impressive 4.6. The life was laidback, featuring long lunches and late dinners with wife Jean and friends, and relaxing by the pool, still wearing his number-7 gold medallion. Laura and Sarah were growing up in a relaxed atmosphere and benign climate.

His interest in football was fitful, though he did retain a video collection of his career. There was the occasional column for the *Sun;* and analysis of German football in the early days of Sky, when Rupert Murdoch's new project was beginning to take off.

For a long while, too, he was co-commentator on ITV alongside Brian Moore at England matches, with a penchant for some foot-in-mouth moments that told of his exuberance. Moore's too. 'Alongside me is Keggy Keegle,' he once said. 'Sorry, Kevin Keegle.'

'They compare Steve McManaman to Steve Heighway and he's nothing like him, but I can see why. It's because he's a bit different,' Keegan once said, for example. And, neatly, 'It's like a toaster, the ref's shirt pocket. Every time there's a tackle, up pops a yellow card.'

Years later, the sensitive, late lamented Moore would regret putting Keegan on the spot when England were in a penalty shootout in the 1998 World Cup. As David Batty walked up to take his spot-kick, Moore asked Keegan if he thought Batty would score. 'Yes,' replied Keegan. Batty missed.

To those beset by stress, as Keegan had been, his life in Spain of occasional work and mainly play would seem idyllic. Once he's over a period of stress, however, Keegan thrives on activity and challenge. Eventually it palled; eventually, after he'd spent seven years in exile, football's siren voice summoned him again. The only surprise was that it took so long to do so.

His epiphany arrived in another of those Mark Lawrenson moments, when he took a quick but certain decision that he again saw through to its conclusion. He was playing golf at Las Brisas, standing over a shot and finding himself suddenly bored. He realised, quite simply, that he had had enough of this way of life. He was forty years old and felt unfulfilled. He went home to tell his wife, whose father had just had a heart attack. She agreed that it was time to return to England. Besides, the girls were now aged twelve and eight respectively and the couple wanted an English secondary education for them.

Keegan was also developing what he hoped would be a money-spinner, if he could only find some business backers. He had named it Soccer Circus. The idea of a sort of theme park based on football was taking shape . . .

Within six months, the family had found a farmhouse they liked back in their old haunts near Romsey in Hampshire and Jean and the girls went ahead to stay with friends while the house was prepared. Keegan decided to drive home in a Range Rover crammed with family possessions. The decision led to a bizarre and very frightening incident.

According to Keegan's own account, having driven 1,500 miles up from Spain his plan was to sleep on a cross-channel ferry but he got chatting to a Tottenham supporter on board and could not resist talking about football. He subsequently began to doze off at the wheel on the M25. Though only around fifty miles from his destination, he decided to pull off the motorway to get some sleep.

He deemed a lay-by near the motorway close to Reigate too noisy and so found a country road instead. He nodded off, only to be awoken by glass smashing around him. A rock had been thrown at the car, to be followed by someone with a baseball bat hitting him. Fortunately a pillow Keegan had been using deflected the worst of the blow. His attackers demanded his wallet; he handed it over and they fled. Dazed and confused, he made his way to a main road where a passer-by rang for the police and an ambulance. Keegan was taken to a local hospital, where he was given eight stitches in the wound to his head.

It emerged when the police caught the perpetrators that a gang of four young men had stumbled upon a sleeping Keegan and saw an opportunity to make up the shortfall from a drugs deal that had gone wrong. At the end of the ensuing trial, three of them were sentenced to four years each.

The court case, though, did not stop some wild allegations and rumours being repeated. Keegan's car was parked in a spot well known locally to what was in those days still referred to as 'courting couples'. More probably these days it would be a so-called 'dogging' site. The young ages of Keegan's attackers also gave rise to some lurid stories that would continue to surface down the years with the advent of the internet.

'It was a massive story,' says Bob Harris. 'But it happened as was publicly stated. I can honestly say [you can] disbelieve any stories you heard.'

Such is a common refrain from those you speak to who have been close to Keegan. All say that the official version of events is accurate. Had there been anything more sinister, they add, it would have emerged by now from someone breaking ranks.

Harris insists that Keegan in his close experience was never involved in anything either scandalous or salacious, despite the pair's time on the England beat being in a climate in which it was quite easy to get away with things.

'I was one of the few that was accepted with the players in the time that I was with England and I would go out with them on the razzle after games and on tours, because you did that in those days,' he says.

'I remember after an England game where they had had a good 4–2 win in Barcelona going out with ten players down the Ramblas. It is inconceivable now that ten England players would do that on the night of a match and no chance of them all falling about on Rioja.

'In those days players didn't get the money they do now and it was beer rather than Kristal but I am sure they had a better time than they do now. You could pick your friends; if you liked someone, you went out whether it was a journalist or a footballer.

'There were some naughty boys around in those days but Kevin wasn't one of the wild boys at all. A lot of them went out and had a high old time but not him. I never once saw him misbehave.

'He was decent company and very dedicated. I was in circumstances with him where girls would target him but when he was ready to go, he went and he went on his own. In those days, a lot got away with it but he didn't mess around.

'There were always whispers but people used to conjure up things for him because they had nothing on him.'

It was certainly a rude welcome home for Keegan, not just a physical shock but also an emotionally disturbing one with all the gossip and innuendo that surrounded him and the incident.

Fortunately for him, there was a happier welcome not too far around the corner and one that would ensure that he did not come to regret his decision to return to England.

7

The Second Coming

Newcastle United were a shambles by the early nineties, life being once again either black or white for them. Bust followed boom; the politics of the club had taken over as the main game in town and their economics were those of the madhouse. Just the usual cycle, then.

After Keegan's exit following that glorious promotion season of 1983–84, Arthur Cox, astonishingly, went too, apparently feeling upset by the board's decision to give him only a three-year contract. He was snapped up by Derby County, where he stayed for nine years; during which time Newcastle three times asked him to return, and three times he denied them.

For a short while in the immediate aftermath of the departures Newcastle even prospered in the top flight. Jack Charlton, prior to his Republic of Ireland exploits, was now the manager and rehearsing his brand of football, euphemistically labelled 'direct', on Tyneside. Newcastle's success lasted about half a season, until teams worked them out and they slipped to fourteenth. Fans did not like the style of play, nor the sale of Chris Waddle to Tottenham at the end of the season; and Charlton walked out.

Coaching lieutenant and former goalkeeper Willie McFaul was promoted but Newcastle trod water, despite the emergence of Keegan's boot-cleaner, that lad called Paul Gascoigne, who had turned into an outrageously talented new sensation. It remained a selling club: Peter Beardsley went to Liverpool for a then British-record transfer fee of £1.9million in 1987; Gazza to Spurs for £2.2million a year later.

McFaul departed early that season after a poor start. Jim Smith came in but he could not turn the tide and Newcastle were relegated in what was a grim season for the region's football. The legendary Jackie Milburn died of lung cancer in the autumn of 1988; former manager Joe Harvey – who had won the club's last trophy, the European Fairs Cup, precursor to the UEFA Cup, in 1969 – four months later of a heart attack.

Weary of the decline of the club, a group of rebel shareholders led by one Malcolm Dix enlisted the help of a local property developer and self-made millionaire, John Hall, who was the brains behind the Metro shopping centre at Gateshead and who would later be awarded a knighthood for his entrepreneurial skills. The aim was to take over the club.

The mood of the support was with them, the more so after the sales of players who would go on to be greats elsewhere rather than for Newcastle. Hall took to the task. He sought to buy shares but found them hard to come by as the board of directors dug in against him. The club's chairman, Gordon

McKeag, was a decent enough man, loved his football and served on the board of the Football League, but he was fiddling as St James' burnt; this at a time when the game in England was on the threshold of changes that would be far reaching and permanent.

That April of 1989, ninety-five Liverpool fans died in the Hillsborough disaster, crushed amid overcrowding at the fenced-in Leppings Lane end of the ground just before the scheduled kick-off of the FA Cup semi-final against Nottingham Forest. It would spawn the Taylor Report, whose main recommendation was all-seater stadiums.

The following summer Gazza wept during England's defeat on penalties in the World Cup semi-final against Germany, but the whole experience proved unexpectedly redemptive. From the nadir of Hillsborough, football would haul itself out of its trough thanks to the tears of a Geordie boy. Soon would come the Premier League as Rupert Murdoch and Sky scented a business opportunity, backed by a number of forward-looking big clubs. Newcastle United were not among them, were not in a position to be among them. They were now in the Second Division.

Peace broke out for a while in the Newcastle boardroom at the turn of the decade, when the two factions accepted that the club was being damaged by the power struggle and Hall accepted a place on the board. Results in the Second Division were promising and manager Jim Smith mounted a promotion challenge. It was crack-papering. All the resentment surfaced when Newcastle lost to Sunderland in the play-offs and there was a pitch invasion that provoked a Football League inquiry.

A share issue flopped and was withdrawn. McKeag stood down; as did Hall, whose son Douglas replaced him. The club was floundering – a fact that was reflected in a lower mid-table season under Smith, who realised that he was losing the board's confidence and resigned in March 1991.

The new chairman, Gordon Forbes, appointed the Argentine Ossie Ardiles as Smith's replacement but this recruitment was doomed to fail. The genial, well-liked Ardiles had been making an encouraging managerial start at Swindon. At Newcastle he blooded youngsters with talent but who struggled to defend, as a 6–6 draw against Tranmere Rovers in a Cup game demonstrated.

Newcastle had slumped to the bottom of the Second Divison in October and the board knew they had to buy some experience. In December they paid Leicester City £300,000 for striker David Kelly. The problem was that Newcastle owed £5million to their bank and had agreed not to buy any players.

Now the bank wanted their money back. Douglas got on to Daddy, away on a world cruise, and John Hall reluctantly agreed to bale the club out with a cash injection to appease the bank. In return, he now wanted the final say in everything. The old order was swept away and Hall senior became the power at the club. To conduct the daily running of the club he installed Douglas along with Freddie Fletcher, a business consultant he trusted, and a shareholder named Freddy Shepherd. While Forbes and his vice-chairman Peter Mallender remained on the board with their titles, they were all but redundant.

Revolution had begun and by February 1992 the coup was complete. After a 5–2 defeat at Oxford United Douglas persuaded his father that poor Ardiles just had to go. John had, embarrassingly, given an interview that weekend to a Sunday newspaper in which he insisted that the Argentine was safe.

Thoughts of one man in particular often sprung to Fletcher's mind around this time. Newcastle's centenary celebrations were looming and Forbes and Mallender had approached one Kevin Keegan, now back from Spain and living in Hampshire, to see if he'd get involved in golf days and dinners. It was decided within the club, though, that Keegan's presence around the club would not look good inasmuch as it would be a reminder of better times and could make Ardiles feel threatened. When in October 1991 Keegan had made his first trip to St James' since 1984, to see a game against Blackburn Rovers, he had been an object of more interest than the team.

However, Newcastle was clearly much on Keegan's mind, too, at the time. Writing in the *Daily Mail* some years later, their sports editor Lee Clayton recalled an incident from early in 1991 when he was ghost-writing Keegan's column for the *Sun*.

Keegan's wife Jean had been driving Keegan and Clayton from Yorkshire to London for a planned night out at Tramps nightclub, where George Best would be joining them. Clayton was sitting in the back of the car and Keegan was on the car phone.

'Yes, that's right. I'd like to be Newcastle manager,' Keegan was saying. 'I could do it. I know it's a difficult job but I've been there before. I can deal with the expectation and give them the football they crave. If we get it right, it will take off like you've never known.'

When Clayton asked who it was on the phone, Keegan told him that it was Sir John Hall. Then, after a pause, Keegan started to laugh. 'Got you there – just testing, making sure you're on the ball!' he told Clayton. 'Don't fall asleep when you're with me. You never know what might happen next.'

The populist tone of Keegan's foreword to Paul Joannou's book *United, The First 100 Years* had touched a nerve as well. Newcastle, he said, had the best fans in football and this was something that would make him forever optimistic about the future of the club, no matter its travails.

Meanwhile Keegan and a business partner had met with Fletcher to talk about an idea for developing grounds in the wake of the Taylor Report. Fletcher subsequently mentioned Keegan's name to Sir John and Douglas Hall and Shepherd in the context of the managerial role. They asked Alistair Wilson, Keegan's old friend from Scottish and Newcastle, to sound him out.

After the heavy defeat by Oxford United, the following Monday they were meeting with Keegan in London. By the Wednesday Ardiles had been replaced and, after a seven-thirty visit to his home by Fletcher, finally informed of what had been going on. Keegan for his part wished to retain an exit strategy and agreed only to take over until the end of the season. Sir John Hall's assurance that Keegan would be given £1million to spend on new players had convinced him to take the job, but he nonetheless preferred to dip his toes into the water rather than sign a long-term contract.

Why did a man who had said that he would never become a manager change his mind, even if only for the short-term? There was the flattery, the ego-massaging by the board for sure. The money and the prospect of being a hero on Tyneside again at the age of forty-one would also have appealed, as would the opportunity to return to the limelight – for Keegan was an entertainer who had always revelled in being there.

Kenny Dalglish had followed Keegan at Liverpool and now, with the help of Jack Walker's money, was taking his first steps in management, with Blackburn Rovers. Could it also have been the case that Keegan envied him a little? Had Keegan's latterly dormant competitive edge been awakened by the prospect of rivalling, even outdoing the man who had replaced him in Anfield's affection?

Once again Newcastle's support, desperate as they were for a new hero, went ape. Nevertheless for some it may have nagged that this was a man with no managerial experience, who had been out of the game for eight years and had taken very little interest in it during that time, and who thus must have little knowledge of players and potential signings.

'You couldn't get away with it now,' says Bob Harris. 'But it did him good, getting away from it, because he was so intense with everything in his life. I don't know if it did him good as a manager, because he came back not knowing anyone.'

Others may have been bothered by the fact that within days Keegan had taken on as his assistant his old mate Terry McDermott. By Keegan's admission McDermott was fond of a drink (though he got this under control for both Keegan and Newcastle's sakes); and at the time of his recruitment he had been selling hamburgers from a van at horseracing meetings. No one was going to voice doubts, however.

That much was evident at Keegan's first game, against Bristol City at St James'. I was sent up to cover the match for my then employers, the *Daily Telegraph*, and it was indeed a remarkable occasion.

The hard-smoking Nottingham Forest and Everton maverick Duncan McKenzie once described Keegan – with a touch of envy at his work ethic if not his comparative talent – as the Julie Andrews of football. That crisp, sunny, February Saturday the Cheviot Hills were certainly alive with the sound of Keegan's return.

I remember the atmosphere and ironies of the day. The railway station was teeming with black-and-white replica shirts, the *Evening Chronicle* was running 'Special K' items on its front page as well as its back. An hour before kick-off the queues were snaking at the foot of the Gallowgate End, which back then comprised terracing whose contours and greenery gave an impression of the Hanging Gardens of Babylon. That was once one of the seven wonders of the world, like Newcastle's role in English football. Now the club was a Tower of Babel. How curious it seemed that there was an office here advertising Newcastle United Financial Services. This from a club then a huge £6.5million in debt. Gallowgate was named after its former use as a site for public executions. You wondered if much had changed, given the number of Newcastle managers who had come and gone in quick succession.

This time there was no helicopter. Club officials had wanted one but Keegan had deemed this a day for the players. Only the scoreboard, advertising £7.99 'Welcome Back Wor Kev' T-shirts, and a gaggle of photographers around him as he took his place in the dug-out told of the fuss.

The crowd was 29,263 strong. The previous home gate, against Charlton, had been 15,663, so Keegan's arrival had immediately brought in £118,000 of increased revenue. With the game goalless at half-time it still looked like familiar dross. Then seventeen-year-old Steve Watson set up a goal for David Kelly to send the fans wild and Liam O'Brien soon added a second. Finally Gavin Peacock sealed a 3–0 win.

'Bill Shankly used to tell me at Liverpool to go out and drop a few hand grenades out there,' Keegan said afterwards. 'I told Peacock to do the same.'

Keegan was instantly quotable and came across as fresh, positive and honest. 'This is the first letter of the first word of the title of the book,' he said. He had spoken during the week about the snowball needing to gain momentum – so, had it? 'Well, it's started snowing.'

He added: 'I felt elated from the word go, even if I haven't slept for three nights.' He then got carried away, as he would prove himself prone to do. 'It's nearly as good as playing. We had fifteen minutes today as good as anything they can ever have seen.'

What was it like on the bench? 'You sit and pretend you know what you are doing.' And what had he said at half-time to inspire the three goals in eight minutes? 'Not a lot. Too much has been said this week. I didn't want to fill their heads with too much.'

It was an uplifting day but there are no happy-ever-afters in football. It is a transient game, which sees people falling in and out of love, worrying and wobbling all the time. The following week Newcastle went to Dalglish's Blackburn and lost 3–1. They proceeded to lose only one more in eight games, but their subsequent five-game losing streak saw them back in the mire. Among these defeats was a 6–2 at Wolves, following which Keegan was charged with misconduct by the FA for comments to the referee and was fined £1,000.

Keegan needed to act. He wanted to sign a midfield player by the name of Darren McDonough, from Luton, but ran into

HEROES

Welcome to My World – Keegan is shown round Anfield by his mentor Bill Shankly

Uncle Joe – With England caretaker manager Joe Mercer at Belgrade airport, where Keegan was assaulted by Yugoslav officials

1

2

3

HAIRCUTS

1 Long And Straight – At Scunthorpe. (Keegan is on the second row, second from the left)

2 Mr Sideburns – Against Newcastle in the 1974 FA Cup final

3 Mulleting It Over – Warming up with Hamburg

4 Getting Big – Sporting the perm at Southampton

5 And Bigger – The power perm for England

6 The Perm Is Turning – Slightly straighter (with even the first hint of grey?) at Newcastle

4

6

1

2

3

1 Dirty Berti – Borussia Mönchengladbach's Vogts bringing down Keegan for the penalty as Liverpool win the 1977 European Cup

2 Captain Kev – Against captain Kenny, Dalglish that is, his successor for Liverpool, in the England vs. Scotland fixture

3 Goal Man – Scoring for England, against Denmark

4 Do As I Say – Keegan the Green Cross Code man, promoting road safety

5 Splash It All Over – Sparring with Henry Cooper, his co-star in the Brut advertisements

6 Back In Toon – On his return to St James' Park as manager in 2008

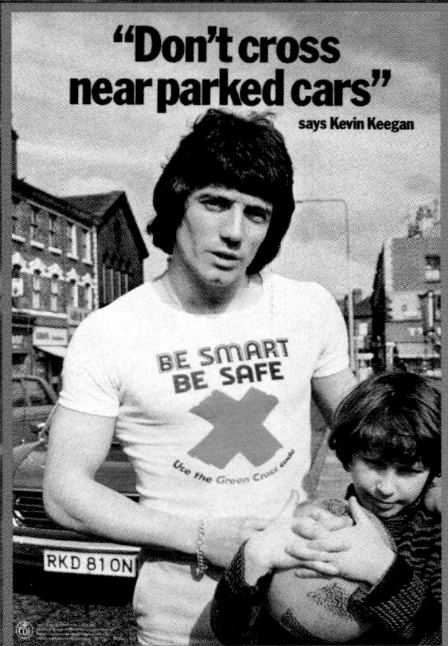

5

6

1

2

3

4

LOWLIGHTS

1 Record Breaker – Head Over Heels proved more top of the flops than Top of the Pops

2 Scars of Battle – Painfully grazed after coming off his bike on the TV show *Superstars*

3 The End With England – Keegan screws his header wide against Spain at the 1982 World Cup

4 Hating It – During that 'love it, love it' television rant against Sir Alex Ferguson and Manchester United

5 Auf Wiedersehen Kev – Keegan and Mike Ashley did not see eye to eye. The fans made it more than clear whose side they were on

5

Marriage Lines – With wife Jean on their wedding day

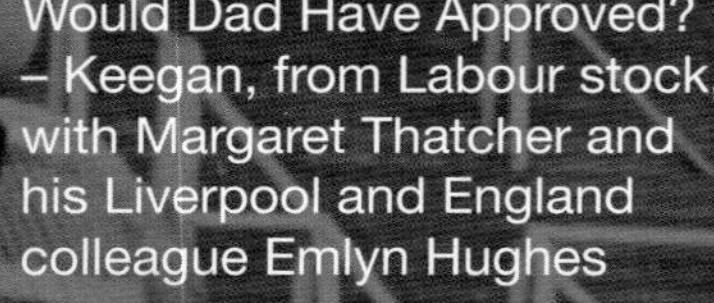

Would Dad Have Approved? – Keegan, from Labour stock, with Margaret Thatcher and his Liverpool and England colleague Emlyn Hughes

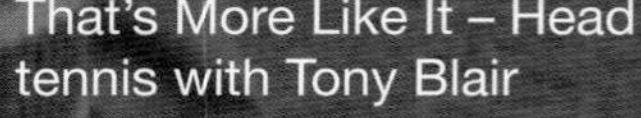

That's More Like It – Head tennis with Tony Blair

a brick wall within the club when he asked for the transfer money. Keegan had been disgusted by the state of the training ground when he arrived – 'Look at the muck,' he'd exclaimed – and one of his first acts was to have the dressing-rooms fumigated. Now he was disgusted by what he saw as a stench in the boardroom.

He resolved to quit but was persuaded by Terry McDermott to oversee a game against Swindon first. Famously Keegan described the club as 'not like it said in the brochure' and headed for Hampshire. This prompted an equally famous phone call from Sir John Hall to Keegan.

'There are only two people who can save Newcastle United Football Club,' he announced. 'And we are talking on the telephone.'

Two things emerged during that call. First, that Hall himself had quite an ego – as those journalists who later covered an astounding 5–0 Newcastle win in a UEFA Cup tie in Antwerp discovered when he hung around the press box keen to be interviewed in the aftermath of the performance and amid the glory. Second, that he knew how to play to Keegan's sense of his own significance.

Keegan soon signed McDonough and, more significantly, centre-half Brian Kilcline for £250,000 from Oldham Athletic, who was big and bearded and looked like a heavy-metal star. Keegan struggled to attract others to Newcastle – and to unload many of his existing failing squad – before the transfer deadline, however. Ultimately it was a close-run race:

Newcastle survived on the last day of the season by winning 2–1 at Leicester thanks to a last-minute own goal.

Finally that summer Newcastle's boardroom power struggles ended, though not before one last bout of blood-letting. Keegan's arranged tenure had come to an end and he was presented with a contract that required him to sell players in order to get any money to buy new ones. He felt insulted by the proposal and walked away, again. George Forbes and Peter Mallender then left the board, leaving the Halls, Shepherd and Fletcher holding total sway; Keegan, with the promise of plenty of money to spend, signed a three-year contract.

Everything turned around. He brought in such proven competitors as Kevin Sheedy, Barry Venison, Paul Bracewell and John Beresford and Newcastle began the season with ten straight wins. This was precursory of a jubilant Championship-winning season, during which Keegan strengthened the side in readiness for the Premier League. He recruited Scott Sellars, Rob Lee (the Charlton midfield player convinced by Keegan's tenuous argument that Newcastle was closer to London than Middlesbrough, who also wanted him) and a striker making a name for himself in Andy Cole, for £1.5million from Bristol City.

The business of making signings offers many examples of Keegan's intuitive management. He apparently once went to scout a player and during the game's warm-up said to Terry McDermott, 'He doesn't run right. Come on, we're going.'

Andy Cole was ineffective when Keegan went to see him play but Keegan signed him anyway, having discovered that Cole was playing with an injury and concluded that he must be a good team player to battle on regardless. Keegan also believed that Lee's range of passing would make him better suited to central-midfield, rather than on the right where he had been, and successfully converted him. This echoed Bob Paisley at Liverpool, who improved the performance of the striker Ray Kennedy by putting him in midfield.

On the season's final day Cole scored a hat-trick as Newcastle thrashed Leicester 7–1. Keegan aimed a message at Sir Alex Ferguson and Manchester United in his programme notes. 'Watch out, Alex – we will be after your title.'

Not quite, but nearly. The following season started unpromisingly. Ossie Ardiles was now Tottenham Hotspur's manager and brought his side to St James' on opening day for a personally enjoyable 1–0 win. After that, though, Keegan's side played an eye-opening, eyebrow-raising season and finished a remarkable third – thanks in part to results that Keegan must have found gratifying, such as wins over Liverpool by 3–0 at home (in which Cole scored a hat-trick) and 2–0 away.

This was the start of an astonishing era both for Newcastle United and the English game. St James' new Sir John Hall stand was erected, increasing capacity to 37,000. Newcastle were spending big on players – among them Peter Beardsley, who returned from Everton for £1.5million in spite of Hall's doubts about granting Keegan the money for the player, who was by this time aged thirty-two.

Keegan was by now living in a grand house on the Wynyard Estate owned by Sir John Hall. Naturally he got his way, as he did in everything. After all, he was now armed with a previously unheard-of ten-year contract as a mark of loyalty by the directors. Arthur Cox returned after his departure from Derby County to join a staff that was burgeoning; Keegan was flanked by McDermott and his trusted first-team coach Derek Fazackerley, the former Blackburn defender whom he saw as a good foil for his own attacking instincts.

There would be spats with players during his reign but none would really question whether or not Keegan was in the right. He was, quite simply, always right. Lee Clark was dropped for showing petulance in response to being substituted; John Beresford was dragged off for daring to question the manager's judgement in a very public exchange of touchline views during a home game.

Even Andy Cole felt the lash of Keegan's tongue and was publicly criticised after doing a disappearing act. He told Keegan that he felt homesick. Keegan quickly met with him and his agent, Paul Stretford (who later represented Wayne Rooney and figured in Keegan's career again too), and the rift was healed. For now.

Keegan also banned a journalist, Tim Taylor from the local morning newspaper the *Journal*, having taken exception to something he wrote. Keegan won the fight and Taylor was sent off to cover Sunderland. Keegan's power extended wide.

The indulgence he received was all because of the football Keegan's team was playing: quick, slick, entertaining and exciting. It became a pleasure to be assigned to St James' and Keegan's popularity spread out into the country. During that 1993–94 season the England team failed to qualify for the World Cup and the manager, Graham Taylor, consequently lost his job. Keegan was suggested as a replacement but he was not yet ready. Newcastle had finished in their highest League position since winning their only title, in 1927, and he wanted to bring home another.

The performance that last season would be a hard act to follow but, buoyed by the signing of the elegant Belgian defender Philippe Albert, Newcastle looked as if they could take the next step at the start of the following season, 1994–95. They won their first six games and were confirmed as the nation's favourite team, the cavaliers, while Manchester United were now viewed with widespread distaste. The latter's reputation had taken a dive thanks to the snarling image created by Roy Keane and company, though there endured a grudging respect and admiration for the relentless achievements of Sir Alex Ferguson's side.

However, as if to prove that you can't please all of the people all of the time, certainly not in football, the grumbling soon began. Newcastle were too open to win titles, went the criticism. They may know how to attack, but they concede too readily. Keegan's £2.7million signing from Queen's Park Rangers, Darren Peacock, was ridiculed at the heart of their defence. Keegan just could not find defenders in the way he could recruit attackers, went the line. There was truth in it all but it seemed churlish to dwell on it, so pleasing to the eye was the team.

'The Geordies like to see a good game,' Keegan later said. 'They don't want to see their team win by playing boring football. They are very unusual in that respect. My job as manager was to put on the pitch what they wanted to watch.'

Newcastle eventually finished sixth that season. Before that, as title hopes began to slip away, Keegan did something that was quite extraordinary and that reverberated through a stunned English game.

In January 1995 Keegan, powerful in the knowledge that his board would acquiesce in any decision he wished to make, was seeking to freshen his squad. He rang Sir Alex Ferguson to enquire about the availability of a right-winger by the name of Keith Gillespie. Ferguson, ever the opportunist, recognised the moment as being similar to the time an enquiry from Leeds manager Howard Wilkinson about Denis Irwin had resulted in Ferguson recruiting Eric Cantona.

The Manchester United manager needed a striker. His first choice was Nottingham Forest's Stan Collymore but the Forest manager, Frank Clarke, was refusing to take his calls. Ferguson told Keegan that he could have Gillespie – if Cole was part of the deal.

Ferguson was chancing his arm. Cole had scored forty-one goals the previous season, another remarkable twenty-seven so far this season, and was the focal point of the Newcastle attack. To Ferguson's astonishment, though, Keegan agreed. The Newcastle manager was coming to the conclusion that in the longer term they were not going to win the title with him. He believed that the team had become too predictable, too geared around supplying Cole, and that their opponents had started to work out how to defend him. Newcastle needed to pose fresh problems for their rivals. And Newcastle would get £6million plus Gillespie for Cole.

Tyneside was first baffled then outraged by the breaking news and a sizable crowd soon gathered outside St James' to voice their discontent. Newcastle had always been a selling club – Waddle, Beardsley, Gascoigne – and now their top goalscorer, the type of Number 9 after Jackie Milburn and Malcolm Macdonald that they had always loved, was going. After the last few glorious seasons it was back to the future. Keegan had led them up the garden path only to leave them panting at the door without even being invited in for coffee.

The Arsenal manager of the time, George Graham, had a saying: 'Never explain, never justify'. He said, 'Your friends don't need to hear it, your enemies won't believe it.' You couldn't picture him doing what Keegan did next, nor would Ferguson have entertained the thought. Suddenly Keegan appeared on the steps to confront the crowd.

He told them that there was method in his apparent madness, that they would be getting a top young winger called Keith Gillespie as part of the deal. The fans were not impressed. They needed to trust him, he said. Look what he had done so far. He would be buying players, he insisted; they would be challenging United for the title. Gradually the crowd was appeased, illustrating the astonishing persuasiveness and charisma of the man at the time. All the same, they had suffered years of heartache and false dawns. It was not Keegan they mistrusted; it was Newcastle United.

Just as he knew what kind of football these fans liked, so he knew what kind of approach they appreciated. 'I treated them in the way they deserve to be treated and kept them informed of what was happening at their club,' he would later say. 'That is the key to their hearts: they don't want to be lied to or deceived. They appreciate honesty in other people because they are so honest themselves.'

That summer Keegan was as good as his word to those fans and spent £14million on three major signings, in the defender Warren Barton from Wimbledon, winger David Ginola from Paris St Germain – the Frog on the Tyne, as he became known – and, as direct replacement for Cole, the muscular Les Ferdinand from Queen's Park Rangers.

'I only signed for Newcastle because of Kevin,' Ginola recalls. 'He was my hero when I was very young. I remember him playing for Liverpool against St Etienne in 1976. He was the start of me thinking I want to be a football player, I want to be a professional footballer.

'When I had a phone conversation with him about going there it was all my boyhood dreams coming true, going back to when I was nine years old. It was just great. I came off the phone thinking, "Wow, Kevin Keegan." I rang my father afterwards and I said, "Dad, I spoke to Kevin Keegan and he wants me to sign at Newcastle."'

Though less impressionable, Ferdinand quickly felt the Keegan charisma too. 'I'd spoken to a few clubs but after five or ten minutes with Kevin Keegan my mind was made up,' he said. 'He told David Ginola and Keith Gillespie, "Supply him with crosses because he's the best header of a ball in the country." He made you feel ten feet tall when you walked out of the tunnel.'

Now Newcastle were ready to come after Manchester United and the 1995–96 season would prove one of the most memorable and thrilling in the English domestic game's history, with a title contest to match.

Newcastle produced some astonishing football in the first half of the season, winning nine of their first ten games. Ferdinand went on to score twelve goals in eight games. Even a 2–0 defeat at Old Trafford in the last game of 1995, in which Andy Cole naturally scored against his previous club, seemed to matter little. They were still seven points clear at the top of the table at the turn of the year.

'I signed on the fifteenth of July and I was voted Player of the Month for the first month of the season,' remembers Ginola. 'People had said it was not the League for me so I quickly shut them up. St James' Park at that time was amazing. Great games, scoring goals every game, great football. Peter Beardsley, Les Ferdinand, Philippe Albert, Rob Lee, Darren Peacock, Robbie Elliott, John Beresford. It was great. We were scoring for fun. Every time we got in the box we seemed to score.

'Kevin was just a great person to work with. He was a manager with a lot of integrity and always treated people well. He was always very available to talk to. It was lovely to work with him every day. Training was done in a good spirit. We worked hard but it was always with a smile on your face.

'Coming from Paris, it was difficult for me in terms of adjusting to a new life. I remember the North Sea. I remember going to Whitley Bay and eating fish and chips with my kids. I told my kids we were going to the beach. They were used to St Tropez! It wasn't easy for someone from the South of France, who'd lived four years in Paris and had a great life, to sign for Newcastle. As a club it was fantastic but it was difficult for my wife and family to settle.

'Fortunately I met some great people up there who helped us; and my life on the pitch and training ground was great. The people involved with Keegan, like Terry McDermott, were very nice and very competent.'

In such an environment the players flourished. By 20 January the lead at the top was twelve points and the title would surely be theirs. The feeling was reinforced when Keegan – clearly acting on the Shankly principle of buying when you are strong – bought a new striker; to ease the pressure, he said, on Ferdinand. The Colombian Faustino Asprilla cost £6.7million from the Italian club Parma but there would be a higher price to pay. The authoritative North-East football writer Alan Oliver described Asprilla's career as embracing 'guns, drugs, bar brawls and porn queens. And that was on a quiet day.'

At first all was well. Though barely bedded in, Asprilla produced two flashes of skill to lay on goals and win the game at Middlesbrough when Newcastle had been trailing 1–0. But the balance of the side was looking different, notably in a 2–0 defeat at West Ham. At Manchester City Asprilla was sent off for a headbutt on Keith Curle as Newcastle lost again. Now the gap was down to four points. And Manchester United were coming to Toon.

Keegan had bought again: David Batty, from Blackburn for £3.75million, as a holding midfield player to protect his back four. Ultimately it came to nought. After battering the United goal, only to find Peter Schmeichel in inspired form between the posts, Newcastle succumbed to a sucker punch on the break when Eric Cantona poached the game's only goal – as he had been doing regularly of late – to whittle into Newcastle's lead.

Suddenly, watching Newcastle and the title denouement over the next few weeks was like watching in slow-motion a sleek Ferrari hitting a wall.

There was an incredible match – certainly the most vivid of all League matches since the inception of the Premier League in 1992 – when third-placed Liverpool at home won 4–3 a game that Newcastle had led 3–1. The sight of Keegan's head slumped over an advertising hoarding as Stan Collymore grabbed the dramatic late winner still plays in the mind's eye.

In hindsight, this was the night that the title slipped away. There were still chances, though; for example, when United lost unexpectedly at Southampton – one of Keegan's old clubs doing him a favour. One suspects that even Keegan knew the game was up, with his own side struggling for form and results. And his anger and frustration at the evaporation of the team's lead at the top all came out in a famous night at Leeds.

Manchester United had, a few weeks previously, narrowly beaten underachieving Leeds. Sir Alex Ferguson, master of psychology in title run-ins to Keegan's novice (at least as a manager), suggested that he hoped Leeds would put in the same effort against Newcastle in a forthcoming game. He also noted that Newcastle had agreed to play in a testimonial for the Nottingham Forest stalwart Stuart Pearce soon after their penultimate game of the season – against Forest. The implication was that, in gratitude, Forest might be tempted to take it easy in return.

Newcastle beat Leeds 1–0 but the night became better remembered for Keegan's post-match outburst live on Sky, headphones on in the Elland Road tunnel, when questioned by anchorman Richard Keys and analyst Andy Gray back in the London studio. The interview went as follows:

KEEGAN: I think things have to be said . . . I think you've got to send Alex Ferguson a tape of this game, haven't you? Isn't that what he asked for?

GRAY: Well, I'm sure if he was watching it tonight, Kevin, he could have no arguments about the way Leeds went about their job and really tested your team.

KEEGAN: And . . . And . . .We . . . We're playing Notts Forest on Thursday and he objected to that. Now that was fixed up four months ago. We were supposed to play Notts Forest. I mean that sort of stuff, we . . . It's been . . . We're bet–. . . We're bigger than that.

KEYS: But that's part and parcel of the psychological battle of the game, Kevin, isn't it?

GRAY: No, I don't think so.

KEEGAN: No. When you do that, with footballers, like he said about Leeds. And when you do things like that about a man like Stuart Pearce. I've kept really quiet but I'll tell you something. He went down in my estimation when he said that. We have not resorted to that. But I'll tell you. You can tell him now if you're watching it, we're still fighting for this title and he's got to go to Middlesbrough and get something and I tell you honestly, I will love it if we beat them, love it.

KEYS: Well, quite plainly the message is: it's a long way from over and you're still in there scrapping and battling and you'll take any of these as long as you continue to get results.

KEEGAN: I think football in this country is so honest and so . . . Honestly, when you look sometimes abroad, you've got your doubts. But it really has got to me and I, I, I've not voiced it live, not in front of the press or anywhere. I'm not even going to the press conference. But the battle's still on and Man United have not won this yet.

A few days later, however, they had all but done so. Newcastle could only draw 1–1 at Forest, which meant that they went into the season's final day trailing United by two points. Newcastle then drew again, at home to Tottenham, while United won comfortably at a feeble Middlesbrough – managed by former United legend Bryan Robson – who succumbed too readily for Tyneside's liking. Keegan made nowhere near as much of that as Ferguson had made of the Forest link, though. Newcastle had failed, albeit gloriously, and the inquests began.

Theories and opinions abounded. It was said that Keegan's Elland Road outburst, growing more vociferous as he warmed to his theme and was unable to hear himself with the headphones on, was the sign of a man who had lost the plot and consequently transmitted anxiety to his team.

Interestingly many of his team later voiced their admiration of him in light of his emotional reaction and honesty. Those who didn't take the game too seriously quite simply enjoyed the entertainment and saw the funny side of it.

As for blowing the title, Keegan had stubbornly refused to bolster the defence when he could. He had desperately (and with warped reasoning) wanted to win it with beauty, to set a new benchmark in the English game. The way he saw it, Newcastle's loss could be put down not to any tactical flaws or defensive shortcomings but rather to the players growing nervous, making uncharacteristic errors.

David Ginola's viewpoint confirms this to be the case but he adds something intriguing to the debate that still goes on to this day. 'The game at Liverpool, that was the start of the worst,' he says. 'We should have won that game – 3–1 up at Anfield with twenty minutes to go. If we hadn't lost that game I believe we would have won the title. After that game we were not so sure of ourselves. It was difficult after that to cope, especially if we went a goal down. We were not so secure inside.

'We went down and Keegan went down as well when he lost the plot with Fergie on TV – "I'd love it, I'd love it". We saw Keegan change. His fight with Ferguson; he was fighting with him. In training it became difficult. Something changed. He was only fighting against Alex Ferguson and Manchester United to prove that he was a better manager, we were the better team. It was one against one. He wasn't competing against all the teams in the Premier League. It was competition between two teams and we lost by four points at the end.

'It was a shame for us, but mostly for the fans and the city. I was so frustrated for the fans. Forget the players, forget the manager. It was sad we didn't win the title, mainly for Newcastle.

'Sir John Hall really deserved to win something for the passion and the money he put in. I have a lot of admiration for the man. He was a real gentleman. When I met him and his wife for the first time, it was like meeting the perfect English lord and lady.'

The hangover continued into the summer but Keegan reckoned he could have another tilt at the title with just a bit of fine-tuning in the transfer market. His first job was to turn down a huge offer from Bobby Robson, now manager of Barcelona, for Ginola.

'Newcastle wouldn't put a price on me,' is Ginola's recollection. 'Barcelona went up to £12million, even more. Keegan told me he would never sell me because the year before he had sold Andy Cole to Manchester United and the fans didn't like it. He didn't want the same thing to happen with me.'

Robson turned elsewhere for new recruits – to Alan Shearer, who had made Blackburn Rovers champions a couple of seasons earlier with his leadership from the front. Kenny Dalglish turned him down, via his assistant, Ray Harford. 'Ray said, "Bobby, please don't put it in the paper. We don't want Alan disturbed,"' Robson recalls. 'I think if he had known there was a chance he could have gone to Barcelona he would have taken it. I played too fair.'

Robson looked now to Holland for a striker and instead of the finished article took a chance on a promising nineteen-year-old Brazilian at PSV Eindhoven by the name of Ronaldo. It would of course work out to everyone's benefit in the long run.

As it happened, the current England captain did want a move and the former England captain knew it. Soon Keegan would pull off the biggest transfer coup in English football history with a record-breaking £15million move for Shearer, who wanted his home fans to see him at his best rather than in the final throes of his career.

It was another of those astonishing days that Tyneside was coming to know under Keegan when Shearer – who, fourteen years earlier, had been in the crowd on the day of Keegan's Newcastle debut – was presented to press and public. 'Not bad for the son of a sheet-metal worker,' he told the crowds to huge cheers as Keegan looked on contentedly, with a 'that's my boy' expression on his face.

Once again it looked promising – after they'd got a 4–0 hammering by Manchester United in the Charity Shield out of their system, that is. Newcastle embarked on seven straight wins, the last being a rousing and remarkable 5–0 victory at home to United (which they could have done with some six months earlier), capped by the most delightful of chipped goals from Philippe Albert.

During the previous season Keegan had dug in his heels whenever it was suggested that he needed a specialist defensive coach. Now he took some things on board, at least when the spotlight was off and in his own good time.

Mark Lawrenson, the man who had done much to end Keegan's playing career, was by now working for Sky television and came up to Newcastle's training ground one week to record an interview with Keith Gillespie.

'I saw Kevin, saw Terry McDermott, had a quick cup of tea and schlepped off back to London and edited the stuff,' he remembers. 'On Saturday morning I got a call from Terry Mac. I'm thinking, "Oh no, he's unhappy with something and wants to pull the interview." He puts Kevin on the phone and he says, "Do you want to get back in?" I hadn't really thought about it but he asked me to come up and have a chat about being the defensive coach.

'I went up the next Sunday and watched them beat Man United 5–0. I met him in the office late morning and he asked me if I fancied the job. I said, "Yeah, I do, but I've just started in television and radio and the money's decent so I'm not coming up for three and sixpence." He said, "That's not a problem here. You can have all sorts of stuff in your contract about winning the League because the club's geared to success." I rang him on the Monday and said, "Yes, I'll come."'

Perhaps Keegan was just pandering to both local and national public opinion, however. Lawrenson became more of an observer than participant.

'He said that for the first few months he just wanted me to come with them everywhere, join in the five-a-sides and have a look. A couple of months went by and it was great because I was getting paid to get fit again but I said to him that I was taking money under false pretences.

'He said the movement in the team was not good at the moment and he was more interested in concentrating on that, if it was OK with me. The team was still doing well and I said OK.'

Lawrenson thus had plenty of scope to watch Keegan in action and is glowing in his observations. He recalls one match with the score 0–0 at half-time.

'Ginola was playing on the left, Shearer up front and Ginola kept doing that thing with the ball of cutting inside, looking to cross it, then coming back out. Shearer was going nuts. At half-time Shearer was running off; you could see he wanted to have a word with Ginola.

'I was walking off with Terry Mac and Kevin, and Kevin just stopped us from going to the dressing-room. He said, "Give them a minute."

'We got in there just in time because Shearer was about to lay him out. Then he said, "I'm not running for you all day. You look up and cross the ball and I'll get on the end of it."

'Kevin just walked among them then and said, "All right, lads?" You could tell he had just let them sort it out. And Ginola went out second half and was brilliant and Shearer scored. With things like that, Kevin was cute.

'He was one of the best man-managers that I have ever been around. He was great. He would come in and be great with everybody, not just the players. He would ask the lad on the door how he was doing. We trained at Durham University and he would talk to lads coming to play on the squash courts. He was just very open.

'He spent an awful lot of time with Ginola. Probably too much in hindsight. Ginola was a bit *comme ci, comme ça* at the time. Kevin knew what he was good at and what he didn't want to do and he didn't want to leave it to somebody else.

'He had Derek Fazackerley, Chris McMenemy, John Carver there as coaches. And he had this attitude of wanting them to enjoy it. "If they're enjoying it, they're not worried about things," he would say. He was always jolly, especially Friday mornings before a game. Get the ball out, make them feel fantastic because we need them tomorrow. That was the clever thing about him.

'I remember one day me and Chris had warmed them up and I think Tino Asprilla came in late – shock – and Ginola was giving it the old Catherine Tate "bovvered" and I mentioned to Kevin about them. He said, "I'll take them, give me one of the keepers for a while." He took them away. He messed around with them and probably got more out of them than we could have. That's what he loved.'

Except that Keegan's love affair with the club was beginning to pall. The previous season's anticlimax had taken its toll. He reckoned he had rescued the club and resented the brickbats he received for finishing second, as the inquests lingered, and for signing Asprilla and Batty to disturb the rhythm. It rankled with him that some people had forgotten almost being relegated to the old Third Division.

He was not feeling the intensity of love he believed he deserved. Also, he had been used to having his own way, running the club from top to bottom, with the Halls, Freddy Shepherd and Freddie Fletcher dancing to his tune. Now they were more concerned about a flotation of the club, such being the vogue among big clubs at the time for becoming public limited companies that would make them rich men and bring in capital. Now the key figure at Newcastle was a financier called Mark Corbridge, who had been brought in to broker the flotation, and Keegan resented his growing influence.

He dropped hints with the players after a Boxing Day defeat at Blackburn, part of a run of only two wins in ten matches that saw Keegan back in his gloomy mode. He would, he told them, 'know when it's the right time to leave this place'.

He felt he was struggling to motivate the players any more – indeed, was struggling to motivate himself. The feeling was dissipating. Soon he had entered into an agreement with the board that he would go at the end of the season but it leaked out. On the day that Newcastle played an FA Cup tie at Charlton, the story appeared in the *Sunday Mirror.*

'Kevin seemed OK and we weren't to know he wasn't OK,' Lawrenson recalls. 'After we had drawn 1–1, he came in the dressing-room and asked me to go and speak to the press for him. I thought that was strange. Then he went himself but said very little.'

The board requested that Keegan meet them at Sir John Hall's palatial Wynyard Hall a couple of days later, where they put it to him that the flotation was in danger of being damaged because of Keegan's being part of it: he must sign for two years or go now. He would go now, he said. This time he meant it, this time it was for real. It evoked Bill Shankly finally being taken seriously about quitting at Liverpool.

It had ended in tears. Yet again Tyneside was stunned by Keegan but this time not in the way it wanted. Any attempts to change his mind fell on deaf ears. Keegan was soon out and away, on holiday abroad, hearing a radio phone-in about his resignation as he drove to a Channel port. The prime minister, Tony Blair, paid tribute. Blair was a self-proclaimed Newcastle fan, who had been pictured with Keegan heading a ball in an echo of the earlier picture with Margaret Thatcher. He once said that any amount of world leaders had passed through 10 Downing Street during his stewardship but only Keegan really impressed his kids.

Arthur Cox took over the team, with Terry McDermott. The day after Keegan's resignation Mark Lawrenson took his first defensive training session. He would not stay long, however, with Kenny Dalglish coming in as manager – ironic again. It was not that Lawrenson did not get on with Dalglish;

it was just that the Scotsman had his own defensive theories, rather more developed than Keegan's.

Tyneside was in for a more austere time. Dalglish did take Keegan's side on to be runners-up again, with Alan Shearer scoring twenty-five goals, and to the FA Cup Final the following season. David Ginola knew his time was up – knew it six months after his dream move to Barcelona was refused. He would not be Dalglish's *tasse de thé* and soon joined Tottenham. 'I knew straight away that I wasn't his priority,' says the Frenchman. 'That's why I left. They didn't play me any more. I don't think the fans knew that.'

Generally, once the shock had subsided, the mood was and will always remain one of deep gratitude to and admiration for Keegan in terms of what he achieved and brought to fans' lives. There remains, though, a tinge of regret, even resentment at being left in the lurch, having been so close to ending the club's long wait for a trophy.

North-East sportswriter John Gibson told Newcastle fan Ged Clarke for his book, *Newcastle United: Fifty Years of Hurt*: 'It ended in tears because of Kevin Keegan's personality. He was always going to implode, throw the dummy out of the pram and stomp away with his nappy round his ankles.

'He did it five times at Newcastle United, sometimes when the public didn't realise. That was his Achilles heel. If he'd won the League, it would have been different. There's no doubt that's what knocked the heart out of him but it also knocked the heart out of Newcastle United. We'd have been a different club. We'd have certainly won things since. It was a great tragedy.'

For the rest of us, on the outside looking in, it had been an astoundingly vibrant period to behold and report on, full of fascination and intrigue that had enriched our football-watching pleasure. Probably, given the highs that Keegan had brought, it was always going to end on a low.

In the aftermath of his departure Keegan said that he wanted a break; once more he said that he would not return to management. But he had now tasted the power that comes with running a football club – the money, too: as the Premiership prospered, clubs were finally recognising managers as key figures, and managers had started to earn the sums that players were.

Those who said that Newcastle were the only club for which Keegan would return to the game – and Keegan had said this himself – were wrong. In fact, he had ideas above his previous station.

8

What kind of Fulham I?

Perhaps it has something to do with his background, or with washing those cars for the people who seemed rich to him as a kid in Doncaster, but Kevin Keegan has always been attracted by – seemed almost envious of – a rich man. He has actually been a bit of a sucker for one.

When the wealthy Sir John Hall came calling, Keegan could not resist the combined siren of Newcastle United and the potential rewards on offer from a man who dealt in big sums. Since then the nostalgic view has it that the two were a double act who worked together to make Newcastle one of England's biggest clubs; one of them off the field, the other on it.

After their early alliance the pair were never quite as close as was thought, with Hall leaving the day-to-day running of the club to others such as his son, Douglas, Freddy Shepherd and Freddie Fletcher. Sir John also had a vision of the club as a Geordie Barcelona. He had a point, even if climatic comparisons might be far-fetched. Like Catalonia, Newcastle does seem to represent a region apart, both geographically and emotionally, from the rest of the nation.

Hall also wanted the football club to be the focal point of a sporting empire that encompassed Rugby Union, basketball and ice hockey. Keegan did not see it that way. He was a football man, knew that the place was a football city, and did not like other activities intruding, diverting some finance here and there, or occupying club officials. He wanted all eyes on the round ball.

Towards the end of his first managerial tenure on the Tyne Keegan grew frustrated at being sometimes unable to contact his board of directors. He grew exasperated at the way the club's flotation preoccupied the power-brokers and to resent being sidelined when it came to profiting from that flotation.

In negotiating his contract at Newcastle, Keegan had been promised £1million when the club floated and duly, eventually, received it. But he was unhappy with the fact that his wages stopped the day he left Newcastle when he had agreed to stay until the end of the season; and, while he kept his club car and phone until he got his flotation money, he was forced to hand over his petrol card and club credit card. This from a club, he would say, where he had played an exhibition match against Liverpool as his farewell in 1984, all the proceeds from which went to Newcastle United.

After tax, Keegan received £600,000 as his cut from the flotation that raised £183million. He viewed with distaste the fact that the board members made fortunes out of a club that he insisted he had done most to build up from a relegation-haunted, second-tier outfit into one of England's most valuable and prestigious. The Halls made £110million.

Thus was Keegan ripe to be caught on the rebound as he looked to recoup what he saw as his losses. After his playing career had ended, with his money well cared for, it took him eight years to get back into the game. Now it took him eight months.

'If Kevin Keegan fell into the Tyne, he'd come up with a salmon in his mouth,' Jack Charlton once remarked. It would be smoked salmon from Harrods Food Hall, actually.

Once he had licked his wounds and counted the cost of his departure from Newcastle, Keegan decided that he wanted to resurrect his already patented Soccer Circus fun-and-learning theme-park idea, which had been mothballed for the last five years. He needed a wealthy backer and approached a man whose fortune and empire may well have been based on borrowed money from banks but who certainly had access to finances. Mohamed Fayed had proved as much in buying the exclusive Knightsbridge department store Harrods and, more recently, Fulham Football Club.

The name of Kevin Keegan opens doors and this was certainly the case with those doors leading to Fayed, who has always demonstrated a fondness for association with celebrity. If Keegan liked rich men, they took to him too. At their meeting in London Fayed was impressed by Keegan's enthusiasm and his project, which he agreed to back. He also said that he wanted Keegan to combine running Soccer Circus with running Fayed's football club.

Keegan was taken aback but has always been open to an offer. He was unwilling to return to the game as a manager just now, so soon after the intensity of his Newcastle experience, but between them they came up with a compromise. Keegan would have a manager working under him and he would run the club, under the title of chief operating officer. This was an altogether more powerful proposition and his penchant for the offbeat challenge overcame him.

It helped that Fayed offered him a financial deal that soothed his pique with Newcastle. The basic salary was £750,000 a year, an astonishing sum for a club in the third tier of the English game and much more than Keegan's wage had been at Newcastle. And, should he stay with Fulham for three years, to the turn of the Millennium, and should Fulham be sold or floated, Keegan would get to own five per cent of the club and stand to make up to £15million.

There was also the chance of success on the field. In fact this was almost guaranteed, as Fayed had a plan to make the Premiership within five seasons and he was prepared to bankroll it. 'I knew that if he wanted success for Fulham the finance would be there to make it happen and I have to be honest, that was the biggest attraction for me,' Keegan later said.

Romantic he may have been in the way he liked to play football, but Keegan had always known the value of money in the game; his experiences as a manager had taught him how directly it contributed to a team's capacity to play the best football.

As a student in London in the seventies I liked to go to watch Fulham, loved the walk along the Thames from Putney Bridge station to Craven Cottage through Bishop's Park, and enjoyed the experience of the average Second Division football enlivened by former England internationals Alan Mullery and Bobby Moore. There was an FA Cup Final appearance, lost to West Ham by 2–0, before George Best and Rodney Marsh arrived to brighten up the scene. It was so much more real, less overwhelming, than Arsenal or Chelsea, Tottenham or West Ham.

Fulham FC may have been situated in one of London's most fashionable areas, amid leafy streets and expensive Georgian properties, but it was an unfashionable, underdeveloped football club, which seemed to be how their supporters – sometimes numbering fewer than 10,000 – liked it. You wondered, therefore, quite what they would make of Keegan's arrival. Decades of mediocrity were suddenly threatened by the promise of excellence. It was all very unnerving.

After all, this was a club that in the days of telexes used to have the address of FULHAMISH. But then, everything they did was Fulhamish. Their Tannoy announcer was the old disc jockey 'Diddy' David Hamilton, best known for his place among the rampant Radio 1 egos of the seventies such as Tony Blackburn and Dave Lee Travis, Noel Edmonds and Simon Bates. Years later, when Fulham did make the Premiership, he was removed from his post in the club's quest for something fresher and more modern. There was an outcry and he was reinstated. Sadly, though, the ladies who used to serve tea and scones to the press from a little kitchen underneath the listed Stevenage Road stand are gone.

I was there at Craven Cottage the day Keegan met the press. For almost two hours he gave interviews to every media outlet that wanted a word. It was virtuoso stuff yet again, full of his customary gusto and enthusiasm, as he outlined the potential of the club. Few could see it; this was no Newcastle and no fans had gathered outside the ground. London was hardly *en fête*. At the end of it, mind, he departed in a limousine waving from the window as he passed pressmen. It was like watching royalty.

There was controversy among Fulham fans: their popular manager Mickey Adams had departed having just got Fulham up from the old Fourth Division, then named League Three, to make way for this new regime. Keegan re-hired his old mentor Arthur Cox to be his own assistant and England team-mate Ray Wilkins as head coach, with Frank Sibley his second-in-command, to prepare and pick the team.

Keegan also hired Alan Smith – neither the former Arsenal striker nor the current Newcastle one, but the former Crystal Palace manager – as head of the Fulham Youth Academy with a brief to bring on their own talent. Smith, who had until recently been managing Wycombe Wanderers, had a reputation for developing kids at Palace, notably among them Gareth Southgate.

Smith had never met Keegan properly but did have some experience of him. At the end of the 1994 season he'd taken his Crystal Palace side up to Keegan's Newcastle. Palace lost and were relegated. Keegan sent down six bottles of Champagne to the team for the long journey home with his commiserations.

'He was genuinely very warm,' says Smith. 'I was a Fulham fan, had been brought up in Fulham and my mother still lived there. My two sons were also Fulham fans and we couldn't really believe it when Kevin went to the club. I remember when I heard, I said, "Don't be ridiculous."

'Then when I got a call from him to offer me a job I was really chuffed. I got a very good salary so Kevin was in my good books from day one. He was really enthusiastic and I liked him straight away.

'He took me to meet the chairman, who didn't speak to me but spoke to Kevin. "Why do we fucking pay him all this money for being director of the youth team? It's too much," he said. Kevin put his arm round me and said, "You told me to go and get the best, so I got the best." When somebody says that to you, you respond. It really did make me feel a part of it.'

And Smith continued to admire Keegan even though the manager thought the academy director should not be driving the sports car he then owned. 'He told me that I had to have something that conformed to my place in the pecking order,' says Smith. Soon a Ford Escort L was delivered.

Suddenly the whole club changed, with Keegan overhauling it from top to bottom as he sought to drag it up by the bootstraps. It was demanding for him, with his wife Jean insisting that the family remain based at Wynyard because their daughters' education was now established in the North-East.

'His working day was unbelievable,' says Smith. 'On Mondays he would get the early train down from Newcastle, do something at Harrods before coming on to the training ground then going back off for meetings again. I can remember him and Arthur Cox running through Bishop's Park after a game to catch a train back North.

'He was always a hundred miles per hour, everything would have to be done quickly. He was a whirlwind getting things done around the place. You had to see the speed Fulham were going at that time. We went from a club that had nothing to the youth team suddenly travelling in the best coaches. He got Adidas to come in and we got the best kit.

'As a youth team we went to Gibraltar for a pre-season friendly and took thirty people. Kevin said with things, "If that's what I want to do, that's what we are going to do." Money wasn't an object at this time. Mohamed wanted it done. They were people in a hurry.'

At first it all worked well. Mostly Keegan set about restructuring a club that was in many respects still amateurish, with the ground in some disrepair and offices dotted around the place from the Surrey training ground at Motspur Park to

Craven Cottage to Harrods. He even began to moot the idea with Fayed of a new stadium, or at the least rebuilding Craven Cottage. Keegan entrusted Smith, who had a background in property dealing, with buying and developing a new training ground.

Smith also had an office at Harrods, along the corridor from Keegan's and next to the one that once belonged to Fayed's son Dodi, who had not long since been killed, along with Princess Diana, in the Paris car crash. Dodi's death had cast a long shadow over Harrods and the club. The arrangement was not ideal for other reasons, Keegan decided, and soon changed things.

'There was a mess-up on the signing of a player and we all moved to Craven Cottage,' Smith recalls. 'The person who made the mess-up went. In fact there was a great turnover of staff in the whole period. Nobody ever stayed for long. It was how the regime was.'

Initially Keegan seemed to work well with Wilkins. He visited the training ground only now and then, working with young players, chewing over the fat.

'Kevin would come down to the training ground two or three times a week,' says Smith. 'A buzz would go round the place – "Kevin's here today." Sometimes he would take the kids and they loved it. He was refreshing, different to what Fulham had been all about.

'We used to have evening training for the eight-, nine- and ten-year-olds and he used to come down for a couple of hours, not every week but quite often. He really bought into the Fulham dream. If you were around it, you were going with it.'

There was, too, a contrast between Wilkins and Keegan, one that almost mirrored them as players. Keegan we knew as darting and buzzy; Wilkins as a midfield man who liked to put his foot on the ball.

'After training Ray would go in the shower and he would take ages,' says Smith. 'He seemed to have a different lotion for his head, his body and his feet and this used to really agitate Kevin. He'd shout, "Ray, come on, I've got to get on." Kevin would come out, put his shirt on with his body still wet and be off somewhere else.'

Keegan and Wilkins had inherited a team that was still adapting to a higher level and was seventh from bottom after three wins from their first eight games under Mickey Adams.

'Mickey was never going to be a big enough personality,' Smith says. 'He would never have gone out and bought the players Kevin did. He was a good, up-and-coming manager and had a good work ethic but Kevin was flamboyant.'

In the background Keegan was buying and selling, hiring and firing. Keegan proved to be unafraid to spend what were, given the level of the club, huge sums of a rich man's money. Ian Selley came from Arsenal for £500,000 and promptly broke his leg. Chris Coleman arrived from Blackburn for £2million, the most ever paid for a player at that level of the game. The transfer came on the recommendation of Smith, who had had Coleman at Crystal Palace. Coleman would himself go on to be a successful manager at Fulham.

'That was something about Kevin,' says Smith. 'He said to me, "I've heard he [Coleman] likes a drink." Kevin wouldn't have anything like that. He didn't like any form of flightiness. "Do we really want him?" He took some persuading but he made him the captain and that really did take us through the division eventually.'

Results came – at one point the team enjoyed eight unbeaten games, six of them wins. But Fulham were not taking the division by storm, as Fayed and Keegan had hoped and perhaps expected. Keegan grew impatient; the relationship with Wilkins grew strained.

Says Smith: 'When Kevin did come down to training, because he was such a name and extrovert personality, it detracted a little bit from what Ray and Frank were doing, because they were a much quieter combination, much less extrovert. I think they always felt happier when he wasn't coming to the training ground.

'Then Arthur would come down. We would put on the training sessions as a staff and he would come over and watch them and you did feel a little bit under supervision. He never said very much but you always felt he would go back and report to Kevin. Kevin didn't seem to make any decision without Arthur.

'The other thing was that the feedback I used to get in the

coaches' room was that Kevin wanted to sign this player and that player, whereas Ray probably wouldn't have signed them. Kevin was trying to stand back but he couldn't stop his enthusiasm. There was Kevin wanting to push on. There was Ray, "Let's do it our way."'

Smith also cites an episode that apparently counted against Wilkins. 'We had a Christmas party which Fayed had arranged and the strain was really telling on Ray. He might even have dozed off at the do. It had really got to him.' The pressure was mounting.

Wilkins did manage to hold on to his job through most of the second half of the season and for a while automatic promotion was even a possibility. But Fulham lost their last three games, slipped from third to sixth and only made the play-offs on goal difference. The inevitable happened. Not many would have bet against Keegan taking over as manager sooner or later. 'Nor could I,' says Smith.

'There was this public opinion. Craven Cottage has got the worst walk-out for a manager, because you have to cross the pitch to get to the dug-out and you could hear it sometimes. There was also this West London thing, because Ray had been at Chelsea and Queen's Park Rangers. They also thought he was a bit dour and he didn't say a lot, unlike Kevin.

'Kevin came to every game at the Cottage and the fans liked him. There was this feeling that, "Oh, Kevin's there, he's up in the stand." Kevin was getting more impatient and he didn't necessarily agree with what Ray did. He would walk down from the stand to the dug-out with twenty minutes to go and you could almost hear them saying, "Well here he comes, he'll sort it out." I really did feel for Ray over that.

'Fulham was full of intrigue at that time and Ray didn't feel he had control. Ray is a very modest bloke and I think Fayed revels in having more extrovert people, people who are more gregarious, around him. Kevin gave him that. I can't say it came as a shock to me when Ray rang and said he had got the sack.

'On reflection, it was never going to work because Kevin has to be the main man and you couldn't stand in his light. It was just the impatience, the enthusiasm. Whoever worked under Kevin, it wasn't going to work. Ray was one of the few easygoing guys it might have worked with. I didn't like seeing it. I didn't like seeing him treated like that; he was treated badly. In the end, I don't think he even got a pay-off. Ray took that badly.'

The change of management did not bring a change of fortune in the play-offs for the team who had finished sixth. Fulham were beaten 2–1 by Grimsby Town on aggregate and faced another season in League Two.

This time, Keegan decided, there would be no slip-ups. Accordingly the pace within the club increased from Wilkins' painstaking through Keegan's brisk to a new manic. Keegan surrounded himself with more of the people he trusted and believed in. He did keep on Frank Sibley as coach. 'The players liked him and Kevin was bright enough to latch on to that,' says Smith.

Peter Beardsley had arrived before the end of the previous season to augment the squad and there were fellow ex-Newcastle players in Paul Bracewell and Lee Clark.

'Kevin liked people around him,' says Smith. 'He saw Bracewell and Beardsley as his lieutenants. They would appease him. In a way, it was a bit disappointing to see. They would all get in the office in the afternoon and have a laugh and they would go and do a bit of shopping for him.'

There would be no brinkmanship next time around. Keegan had the money to recruit and did so. With fire power to spare in Beardsley, Paul Peschisolido, Geoff Horsfield and the German Dirk Lehmann – to whom the crowd took readily because, so we are told, they believed he looked like a porn star – along with Barry Hayles some time later, Fulham waltzed to the title with 101 points. Philippe Albert even came in for a dozen games on loan at the end of the season. The Keegan Midas touch had worked again.

The club became even more of a mad whirl. 'I'd be a liar if I said I didn't get carried away, even though I was only the academy director,' says Smith. It was a whirlwind, a big gush.

'Sometimes the chairman would come down in his helicopter from Harrods or his home in Cobham; and if Kevin ever wanted to use it he would go by helicopter too. That was how surreal it was. It was a really exciting, almost glamorous period.

'It was an interesting place to work and the chairman was a challenging person, an off-the-wall character. Whenever Kevin took a problem to him he would say, "That's not my problem. That's what I pay you for." Every day with Keegan something was happening. I never suffered from boredom.

'Looking back on my three years there, it was a real golden era in the club's history and it always will be. It is a cottage club, if you'll pardon the pun, and Kevin Keegan had an incredible impact at Fulham Football Club.'

By now Fulham were Premier League material; that much was clear at the start of the following season. Keegan brought in big names like Stan Collymore and Karl Heinz Riedle, both clients of Paul Stretford, who had been Andy Cole's agent. Keegan would go on to buy shares in Stretford's Proactive management company and Neil Rodford, the young Fulham managing director to whom Keegan took a shine and who arranged a flat in Knightsbridge for him, went on to become a senior executive with Stretford's organisation.

Fulham went unbeaten in their first ten games, of which they won five in a row, to rise to second in the table. It seemed as if the Keegan miracle-working was set to continue.

They hit a plateau, however: the squad was nearly but not quite good enough and by the turn of the year had settled into that position so tantalising to fans, the fringe of the play-offs. Of course play-offs were invented to tantalise and retain the interest of the fans. Keegan would need to buy again to take the team to the next level and Fayed would have to take some decisions about backing him.

Then came a series of events to interrupt the march and take Keegan's life and career in another unexpected direction. This time he was headed towards the fulfilment of an ambition, into a job he had always coveted and felt he was born to do.

9

Country Manager

The Kevin Keegan story in many ways reflects that of the wider English game of the past few decades. Keegan dragged himself up by the bootlaces from humble, blue-collar origins, worked diligently, through effort and endeavour, to advance himself as a player but was ultimately frustrated at the highest level despite much club success. It was only a matter of time before he became the England manager and had the chance to see whether or not he could change that for the better.

It is usually the case that those chief executives and chairmen in charge of hiring coaches and managers seek to appoint someone who is the very opposite of their predecessor; an antidote to the ills that prompted the sacking or abandonment. Certainly the history of the England team in the 1990s illustrated as much.

At the start of the decade, as replacement for Sir Bobby Robson, Graham Taylor represented the logical conclusion to the direct-style English game of the time. Yet both he and the English presence were found wanting when confronted by the more sophisticated tactical nuances of the international game: after a painful 2–0 defeat in Holland England failed to qualify for the 1994 World Cup in the United States.

Then came Terry Venables, who succeeded in getting the most out of some gifted players – notably Paul Gascoigne – as England reached the semi-finals of Euro '96 on home territory. Just under three years after losing to the Dutch, England beat them 4–1 at Wembley.

Venables was in tune with the development of the modern game and his mobile, adaptable team promised progress. There was, however, an element of East End ducking-and-diving about him in contrast to the decent, upright Taylor. Venables' tangled business affairs received much publicity and adverse comment, with even a *Panorama* devoted to him, and led to scepticism within the Football Association about his integrity. So much so that the FA refused his call before the tournament for an extended contract; Venables felt insulted, said he would see out the summer and then walk.

His successor, Glenn Hoddle, was supposedly clean-cut, loosely described as a born-again Christian and appeared likely to carry on the modernisation programme. Surely he could not possibly embarrass the FA? But he did. In an interview with *The Times* he somehow departed from the agenda to which he was being paid to stick and chose instead to use the platform to air his mish-mash of religious beliefs, making some ill-advised comments about the disabled living out the consequences of former-life events.

The interview sparked outrage and was the final straw for the FA, who had been plunged into turmoil after the 1998 World Cup finals in France – which had promised much but ended in epic defeat by Argentina in the last sixteen.

In conjunction with the FA's director of communications, David Davies, Hoddle had produced a book telling the inside story of the campaign and was roundly criticised for what was perceived to be a betrayal of dressing-room secrets. In the week of the book's release England went to Stockholm and lost 2–1 to Sweden in their opening qualification match for Euro 2000; this was followed by a drab goalless draw with Bulgaria and a streaky win over Luxembourg. As Hoddle began to lose face and matches the word within the England camp was that his players did not warm to him as his dourness of character kept them at too great a distance from him.

To add to this the FA's chairman, Keith Wiseman, and chief executive, Graham Kelly, were forced to resign amid scandal about doing a deal with the Welsh FA for support within UEFA in return for certain favours and financial rewards. David Davies – who had told Kelly at France '98 that he wanted to leave the organisation because it needed to change and was too slow in doing so – became acting chief executive of an organisation that was already in chaos.

'It was a turbulent time for everybody,' Davies recalls. 'Everybody needed a lift, not just the team but the FA as a whole.'

Things started to look up when England had a 2–0 win in

a friendly. Then Hoddle, with his bizarre comments in *The Times*, undermined his own recovery. Even Prime Minister Tony Blair discussed the issue on the ITV morning show with Richard and Judy, prompting the FA to take action.

They wanted Hoddle to hold a press conference to explain and apologise but he refused, preferring instead to do smaller interviews. 'I liked Glenn but I was told from day one that he could be stubborn and that word stuck,' says Davies. Soon Hoddle was conducting a full-blown press conference – to express his anger and pain at his sacking – and we watched him squirm in a farewell appearance at the Royal Lancaster Hotel, just around the corner from the FA's former headquarters at Lancaster Gate in London.

It was January 1999 and England had a crucial European Championship qualifier against Poland coming up in March. The FA needed to act quickly. A small working group of key players from the board and international committee, among them Howard Wilkinson (then technical director), Noel White of Liverpool and David Dein of Arsenal, was established to decide on Hoddle's successor. Wilkinson was to be caretaker for a forthcoming friendly against France and Davies was to be the headhunter for the permanent coach.

Apparently Sir Alex Ferguson had been a possibility before Hoddle: Davies at the time had heard encouraging noises from Old Trafford. This was no longer the case. Manchester United were about to win their amazing treble of Premiership,

FA Cup and European Cup. Neither was Arsenal's Arsene Wenger a real contender, deeply entrenched in club duties as he was. Few Englishmen at the time really appealed. Except one.

'You looked at English options and there weren't many, but the name of Kevin Keegan screamed at you,' says Davies.

He wanted first to check the views of some of the senior players – Alan Shearer, Tony Adams, Gareth Southgate and Gary Neville. 'I put Terry Venables' name forward because I thought he was still the best at that time,' says Adams, who had been captain under Venables only to be deposed under Hoddle by Shearer. 'But I think Kevin got the job because Alan really championed his cause.' It was also because there were several with significant power at the FA who simply would not have Venables back.

One Friday morning at Lancaster Gate the working party agreed that Keegan should be approached, via Fulham and Mohamed Fayed. Davies phoned Laurie Mayer, Fayed's press secretary, with whom he had once worked as a BBC reporter. Within a few hours Davies was making his way through the back entrance of Harrods, up to the fifth floor and through a set of big wooden doors into Fayed's office.

The two men had an amicable chat during which Fayed agreed that Davies could speak to Keegan. The Egyptian was getting some bad publicity at the time because of his involvement with Tory politician Neil Hamilton in the cash-for-questions scandal, and a recent application for British citizenship had been turned down. Quite probably he sensed a chance to improve his image.

Fayed asked Davies not to contact Keegan until after Fulham's FA Cup tie at Manchester United that weekend, then presented him with a Harrods carrier bag containing something heavy. It was a gold bar. 'A gold bar of chocolate,' Davies explains with a smile.

Davies then took a taxi across Hyde Park to Lancaster Gate where just a single TV crew remained on a cold, dark February evening. They did not pick up on the carrier bag he had in his hand.

On the Sunday, it being Valentine's Day, Davies was dining with his wife at London restaurant Scallini's when his mobile phone rang. It was Keegan replying to a message Davies had left shortly after Fulham had lost 1–0 at Old Trafford earlier that day. 'Can't think what you want to see me about,' Keegan said. Davies and Keegan had first met when Davies was a BBC reporter in the North-West covering Liverpool games and Keegan was plying his trade at Anfield. The pair had worked together on a show called *Take Two,* in which Keegan and the then Manchester City chairman Peter Swales talked about their disparate lives in football.

Keegan and Davies agreed a meeting for midday the next day at Keegan's home at Wynyard and Davies rang Howard Wilkinson and Noel White in Sheffield to arrange a rendezvous at Darlington station ahead of the summit. Davies caught a six a.m. train from London.

'We sat in Kevin's front room and he took everyone aback,' says Davies. 'He said he would like to do the job for four games, alongside the Fulham job. None of us had considered that. But I was confident that once we got him in the guy would like the job; once inside the England cocoon, he would enjoy it.'

They agreed provisionally to Keegan's idea, which carried echoes of his baptism at Newcastle when he agreed to take charge until the end of the season. The FA's acting chairman, Geoff Thompson, was visiting Australasia in an ambassadorial role and was quoted as saying: 'It will all end in tears.' Thompson later denied having said such a thing, but in fact he became such an anonymous and peripheral figure within the organisation that nobody much cared about his views anyway.

As the week went on, negotiations were completed in a meeting at the All England Lawn Tennis Club at Wimbledon, despite what Davies describes as some 'bumpy moments'. For Fulham, Neil Rodford sorted out the financial details. Keegan's own were believed to have taken the England coach's salary on to a new level. Venables was thought to be on around £125,000, Hoddle double that. Now Keegan would be not far short of £1million a year, should he come to take the job full-time.

Great patriot though he was, Keegan took a little persuading. He knew the level of scrutiny and criticism to which he and his family would be subjected. He also knew he was on to a good thing at Fulham. His team might have been treading water that season but a push for the Premier League was just a spending spree away. However, this was England and, after his acrimonious exit as a player, it was a chance to return, General MacArthur-like, in glory.

A press conference was called at the Metropole Hotel in London's Edgware Road, during which Keegan duly banged the drum in the way he knows best.

'I know I need people to help me but I don't need a faith healer,' he said, taking a swipe at Glenn Hoddle and his belief in the methods of his controversial aide Eileen Drewery. He then issued a bit of Don Revie, not that too many picked up on it. 'I want all the players to sing the national anthem. I want the same things everyone else wants for England,' he said.

Keegan went on to cite the triumph of 1966 and say how he would love to emulate it. These days we dare not speak its name, the World Cup win having become a millstone rather than an inspiration, a refuge for the nostalgic and deluded that serves only to illustrate how far behind the rest of the world England now are. At the time, after what seemed like austerity under Hoddle, it was what audiences wanted to hear.

'It was one of the longest press conferences of my life but it was fantastic,' says Davies. 'After everything we had been through, it was just what we needed. I was really enthusiastic. Kevin had that effect.'

There were caveats. Keegan had no proper coaching qualifications and it was at a time when France had proved the merit of a well-organised developmental programme that had produced the 1998 World Cup winners. England's response was to appoint Howard Wilkinson as technical director, with a brief to overhaul the coaching system. This was slightly embarrassing.

'Howard did have some concern over the lack of coaching qualifications but he saw that Kevin was the one that could unite everyone,' says Davies. 'I'm not sure who else was in that category.'

There was also the criticism, targeted largely at Davies, of the FA's failure to persuade Keegan to commit to more than four games. For fear of upsetting Fulham Davies could not in his defence convey his belief that Keegan would stay beyond the agreed period. For his part Fayed was by now onside, deeming Keegan's appointment as an honour for Fulham. He had an ulterior motive, too. 'Now can I have my British passport,' he said only half-jokingly.

Alan Smith, who was then at Fulham, reckons there might even have been another thought crossing his mind. 'Nobody wanted to see Keegan go,' he says. 'He had so much enthusiasm. But he was quite demanding and the chairman might have been thinking, "Do we need to do it that way?" – because by that time we were up and running.

'Kevin was spending money and probably there were times when he didn't get his own way and would sulk a bit.

The chairman might have been thinking, "I know a bit more about this football business."'

The FA certainly thought that Fulham's loss was their gain. These were desperate times for them. England, the FA decided, needed less of a technician and more of a motivator if they were to reach the European Championship finals in Holland and Belgium the following year. Keegan was bubbly, approachable and talkative. England needed to draw a veil over the Hoddle era with someone who could inspire the players and excite the nation.

Naturally, Keegan surrounded himself with familiar, favourite faces. There was Derek Fazackerley as his coach, Arthur Cox as his sounding board – though the FA refused to appoint him full-time. Peter Beardsley even joined as a junior cone-carrier, a bridge to the players.

'I found Kevin to be as he played,' says Davies. 'Warm, enthusiastic, alive and vibrant. Humorous too. He looked you in the face.'

Adds Tony Adams: 'I liked him, still do. He is a great bloke, a very warm man. He was very charismatic and determined, a lovable kind of guy.'

Adams also recalls one of Keegan's first acts: the recruitment of a psychologist-cum-comedian called Watt Nicholl ahead of England's game against Poland at Wembley. Self-styled Watt Nicholl MP (Motivated Person) had variously been a folk musician, a speedway rider and the author of part autobiography, part self-help book bizarrely entitled *Twisted Knickers and Stolen Scones*.

'It was a funny psychological book. Kevin brought him in to lecture us,' explains Adams. 'He was quite entertaining and there was a lot of good positive thinking. There was some good stuff in there.' Nicholl, whom Keegan had first encountered some years earlier, described Keegan as being 'like rocket fuel' but was not used again. The new manager knew the ridicule that he could invite in the future even if he would be indulged.

Another England player, Steve McManaman, also spoke of the Keegan effect. 'When Kevin Keegan took over, we had a convivial manager again,' he said in his book, *El Macca: Four Years with Real Madrid*. 'He tried to be friendly with the lads and make things relaxed. We used to have race nights where we would all sit together in front of a big screen showing tapes of horse racing. Keegan or Alan Shearer would be the bookmaker. It was fun and you wouldn't be stuck in your bedrooms, going through the television channels just to alleviate boredom. He liked getting the lads together, having a laugh and a joke with us in training.'

All caught the mood in Keegan's first match, which England badly needed to win to get their campaign back on track. They did. Paul Scholes scored a hat-trick as England won 3–1, fortuitously getting away with a handball for one of the goals. And Keegan, he revealed after the match, had had some advice for Scholes before the game. It could be guessed.

He told Scholes to go out there and drop some hand grenades.

'It was a triumph,' Davies says, recalling too that Fayed had arrived in the Wembley banqueting hall fifteen minutes before kick-off to present Davies with a Fulham scarf that he was instructed to wear. 'Even a manic depressive like me enjoyed that game.'

The inevitable happened. After a draw away to Hungary in a friendly in April, the bandwagon was rolling for Keegan to take the job full-time. Ever vulnerable to flattery and being wanted, he accepted the mission the following month. 'Having done it for two games, I really feel I belong here. I listened to my head,' he said.

'That was instinctive and I was jubilant,' says Davies. 'I'm not sure all the selection committee believed me when I said that he would take to the job.'

Keegan recommended Paul Bracewell as his successor at Fulham, who would finish ninth, but he was soon sacked and the Frenchman Jean Tigana was eventually brought in to complete Keegan's work and take them into the Premiership. 'I don't think it was the most amicable of partings,' Davies says of Keegan's withdrawal from Fulham. 'It's not easy to do both jobs.'

Neither did Keegan's full-time appointment have quite the desired effect of sustaining momentum. England drew their two June qualifiers, against Sweden at home and Bulgaria away, and qualification was on a knife edge.

Come the September and the last two games of qualifying, England comfortably disposed of Luxembourg by 6–0 at Wembley then drew 0–0 against Poland in Warsaw. It was an ironic result. When he took the job Keegan had warned that if the need was for a goalless draw away from home, he was not your man.

The result – or, more accurately, a 2–0 Swedish win over Poland that prompted the thought that Keegan might be a lucky manager – did secure a November play-off to qualify for the finals. It would be against Scotland, over two legs at Hampden Park and Wembley, and England made it through only narrowly, in usual black-and-white fashion – this appropriately enough, given that Keegan had just come from two clubs, in Newcastle and Fulham, who sported the colours. Keegan was hailed as a hero as England won 2–0 away. Four days later, there was Euroscepticism as they lost 1–0 at home. 'That was hairy,' Davies recalls.

The benevolent spin-off, Keegan and England might have hoped, was that expectations were probably lower than they had ever been as England went into a major tournament. Not that Keegan or his players would get away with it that easily, however. England never do.

Form had been reasonable. In February England had drawn 1–1 at home to Argentina and in May did so again with Brazil. There followed two decent, if not wholly convincing, victories over Ukraine at Wembley and Malta in Valletta. England were in acceptable shape.

Aware of the potential for excess among England followers at that time, Keegan and Davies went on public-relations trips to Holland and Belgium. The FA were also concerned about the relatively small stadium in Charleroi where they were scheduled to play two matches. Keegan even visited the battlefield at Waterloo for a patriotic photo opportunity.

'I never quite knew if he enjoyed these things, even though he was somebody who was a gift to PR,' says Davies. 'But he would always put on a show and a performance for you.'

Doubts had been growing, though, after Keegan's sometimes curious selections and tactics. Tony Adams certainly experienced them in the build-up to England's first match, against Portugal in Eindhoven.

'The first team trained against the reserves, who were playing in the formation the Portuguese used, with one striker up and one off,' Adams recalls. 'Kieron Dyer was destroying us and someone needed to get hold of him.

'I said, "Hold on, Kevin, what's going on?" Then Derek Fazackerley walked on to the pitch and had his say. I asked what we were going to do about it. We were a very offensive team, all flying forward with Alan Shearer and Michael Owen up front in a 4–4–2, which was not how many international teams were playing at that time.

'Kevin stood there with his arms folded, letting Derek do his bit and Arthur Cox do his bit. Alan said a few things. Some would say he was confused and didn't know what to do. If Arsene Wenger did it, everyone would say he was a genius. Kevin wanted others to deal with it but I am not sure we all knew what we were doing. It looked to me like he didn't know how to deal with the situation.'

As it happened in training, so it did in the match – although any misgivings seemed to be allayed when England began astonishingly, going 2–0 up in twenty minutes through Paul Scholes and Steve McManaman.

It never looked like a convincing lead or performance, however, and England's midfield became swamped. The paper for the cracks was wafer thin. Goals by Luis Figo and Joao Pinto made it 2–2 by half-time and Soares grabbed what proved to be the winner twelve minutes into the second half. It was a mess, made worse by Liverpool fans among the England support jeering David Beckham. Recrimination began back home. So much for reduced expectations.

'One to one, I don't care how good a defender you are – if you get isolated with someone who has pace you are knackered,' says Adams. 'I always realised that Kevin's teams were never good defensively. I spoke with him about the way he saw defenders, more as individuals and not as units.

'I see defending more as a unit, starting with the front two. The team is a unit and everyone has to put a shift in. I am not sure he saw defending the same way I did and tactically his teams would back me up on that. They were very flamboyant. They move, they attack, they want to get crosses and shots in. Football for me is a balance and they didn't quite get the balance right.'

Adams also laments the lack of instruction about how he and Sol Campbell should best handle the threat of Pinto playing as the striker, with Luis Figo off him.

'When you have got a man running at you, the decision is very difficult. Sometimes you can deal with it, other times you need someone in there sitting. It would have been all right if Kevin had said, "I want you to push in on people, I want you to leave Sol with Pinto," but we were a little bit unclear. His attitude seemed to be, "There's the forward, you're a great defender. Deal with it."'

It is telling that Adams does add that Keegan 'put on some great training sessions for the forwards'.

Adams, then thirty-four, aggravated various injuries and missed the next two games, against Germany and Romania. He watched them from the stand. He also watched as the England camp attracted criticism for the atmosphere that Keegan fostered; amid discontent from media and players, anger grew at the first-game defeat.

The team hotel near Spa, in Belgium, had horseracing from back home piped in via satellite and there were stories of card schools for large sums of money, pots going up to £20,000, though Keegan later successfully sued one newspaper that quoted big numbers and suggested he was involved.

'On one level I felt sorry for Kevin Keegan,' Steve McManaman would say. 'With England you know you are always under ten times more scrutiny than at any other period of your football career. That means you can pretty much dilute some of the wild stories to a tenth of their strength and you may get a truer picture.

'The tales of card schools and gambling under Keegan were so exaggerated. The amounts mentioned were ridiculous. All he did was to come in and try to endear himself to the players, to make it a campaign we were all in together. He wanted to build up team spirit and foster camaraderie and as a player you can only commend that. It is pretty boring being holed up in an isolated hotel in Belgium.'

'Kevin's relationship with the players was very chummy,' says Davies. 'Somebody might have thought he was a senior player. He liked to play cards and that became an issue because of how much time and what money was involved.'

There were also reports that some of the younger players were less than impressed, indeed felt uncomfortable with Keegan sitting at their table during dinner regaling them with tales and the sayings of Bill Shankly, of whom they'd only vague knowledge. This may say more about the younger players, mind, or the ones who were not too fond of Liverpool, than it reflects as criticism of Keegan.

'He was sometimes cross with me that I wasn't more aggressive with the media,' adds Davies. 'My attitude was that I never banned anybody. At the end of the day, there is a rough and tumble here with the media, same as there is in Westminster.'

Adams sought to ignore the goings-on in the camp but knew it was happening. 'There were a lot who liked the racing. Steve McManaman, Michael Owen, Robbie Fowler, Alan Shearer,' says Adams. 'I joined in with race nights to be part of the group but it wasn't my thing. I didn't want to get involved. With Arsene Wenger at Arsenal, it was all about preparation and this was different.'

Some of the stories went away six days after the Eindhoven debacle when Keegan managed to turn the tide with his finest hour as England manager.

It was clear at his press conference, where he gave answers in German, the day before the game against Germany that he was still love in the country where he had played for three seasons. This love diminished a little the following night, however.

It was a poor match, between the two worst teams at the tournament (the worst German side in living memory). It was settled by Alan Shearer's header. Against Portugal Paul Ince had looked baffled by it all going on around him; now he held his own against a team without the same movement.

The mood changed and the next day Keegan was forgiven for much that had gone before as he revelled in the result at a press conference. There was still a touch of resentment towards the media in his voice, however, as he defended his captain, Shearer, who had been sharing some criticism with the manager.

During the conference, Davies was suddenly called away to a meeting of the UEFA executive. Earlier in the week a group of England fans, angry and humiliated at the team's opening defeat, had rioted in Charleroi and Belgian police had turned water cannons on them. Now UEFA were contemplating throwing England out of the tournament. The mood at the morning staff meetings that Keegan attended in Davies's hotel room became less relaxed.

In the end the team solved UEFA's dilemma for them when all the problems came to a head against Romania in the last group match. After the drum-banging something more orchestrated was needed but England just could not hit the right notes. Against expectations Keegan picked Dennis Wise in midfield where England were overwhelmed. Remarkably they did take a 2–1 lead after goals by Shearer and Owen overhauled Cristian Chivu's but Dorinel Munteanu equalised before Phil Neville conceded a late penalty, converted by Ioan Ganea to give the manifestly superior Romanians a 3–2 win that meant that England were going home.

The same thing had happened as against Portugal, with a deep-lying striker in Adrian Mutu taking England to pieces. Mark Lawrenson was co-commentating for the BBC with Barry Davies. 'I said that the little Number 10 playing in the hole was running the game,' he recalls. 'It was so obvious what the problem was but nobody dealt with it.

'I went back and did the highlights programme at night and I said the same thing. It feeds into the England hotel. I heard that Kevin turned to Derek Fazackerley and said, "What a bastard." I saw Faz later at the tournament when he came back to watch a couple of games and asked how Kevin was. He said, "He won't be talking to you in a hurry."'

Lawrenson has since met Keegan on occasions – at for ex-Liverpool players, for example – and shaken nd exchanged pleasantries, he says: 'I won't say I fell ou th him. He fell out with me. He forgives but he is not the kind of person who forgets.'

Angst and inquests would continue. Years later Michael Owen in his own autobiography would question Keegan's judgement and his deployment of the striker. It became embarrassing when Keegan returned to Newcastle, with Owen by now a player there.

The day after the Romania defeat Newcastle's then senior striker Shearer gave a press conference to announce his retirement from international football. And Keegan gave the Sunday newspapers a back-page lead. Apparently, if he didn't get good results from England's first two World Cup qualifying games of the autumn, against Germany and Finland, he would quit.

Keegan met with the staff that day and was, according to Davies, philosophical. After what they had been through with Hoddle there was certainly no talk within the FA of sacking the manager. 'His relationships within Lancaster Gate worked very well,' says Davies. 'He was very visible and the staff enjoyed Kevin.'

By now a new chief executive, Adam Crozier, was in place and Keegan met with him over the summer. Crozier asked if there was anything Keegan wanted; Keegan replied that he would like Arthur Cox to join the staff full-time. It was refused.

'There was a story that Kevin wanted more backing,' says Davies. 'The attitude within the FA was, "Well, how many is he going to bring?" Perhaps some of us should have worked harder on pulling that through. Would it have made any difference? I don't know.'

There was better cause for optimism when England played France, the winners of Euro 2000, in a friendly at the Stade de France in the September. In Shearer's absence Keegan had made Tony Adams captain and changed the static 4–4–2 system that had looked so predictable in the summer.

'We went 4–5–1, converting into a 4–3–3, and played some good football against the World and European champions,' Adams recalls. 'Kevin started with Andy Cole up front and brought Michael Owen on and he got an equaliser. It was different because Alan wasn't there and our focal point had changed. Alan was so powerful and so big. He would never have dropped Alan. He got him the job.'

All bets were off a month later, however, as England and Keegan ran into a German side seeking revenge and redemption after their own summer of misery and soul-searching.

The build-up started sadly and badly for Keegan some ten days before the game, when his mother Doris died. Consequently and on only this occasion he missed a press conference: the one to announce his squad.

Davies feared the worst, therefore, when England assembled on a Tuesday for the Saturday game against Germany. 'But he was fine. He said, "Let's get on with it, it's a big game."'

Keegan's moods are changeable at the best of times, however, and as the week went on he was tetchy as he found himself assailed by the vagaries of grief, his deteriorating relationship with the press and the pressure of the game. He was not best pleased, then, when a press conference turned on him and accused him of misleading journalists by keeping quiet about an injury to Steven Gerrard. He was even angrier that his plan to play Gareth Southgate as replacement in midfield leaked out and was ridiculed on the eve of the game.

'Kevin was furious that Friday night,' Davies says. 'He thought they were arseholes for thinking we were lying. His attitude was, "We are falling over backwards and they are still not satisfied." Then the Southgate stuff was getting out and he rang my room asking what was the point. The pressure on him was enormous.

'On the day of the game I opened the curtains and it looked like the end of the world. It was throwing it down. Kevin came down to breakfast unshaven and looked as if he had been awake all night. He looked awful and started on again about what was said last night.

'He and I went and sat down with a coffee and I said, "Look, just put this out of your mind. What is important is what you do today and we will deal with this afterwards. Just go and show everybody and win this game." You do your best to be supportive.

'We both are quite thin-skinned but I don't apologise for that. I just don't think you need to show it. You read some things sometimes and you want to scream but you don't. Don't believe that managers don't read things, by the way. They read everything, with one exception among them – Sven Goran Eriksson, who genuinely didn't care what they had to say.'

When Davies later saw Keegan in the tunnel before the game, he thought all had blown over except the rain. But the selection and system, a curious one that featured five defenders and five attackers, gave the team a distinct them-and-us feel. Gone was the idea of playing Paul Scholes off a main striker, in was Southgate as a holding midfield player.

'Gareth could have done it but when we have the ball, can he spray it around with that passing range?' Adams says. 'Then, at 1–0 down, you don't need a holding midfield player. It might have been an option away from home.'

England did indeed go 1–0 down, with David Seaman unable to keep out Dietmar Hamann's low free kick that skidded on the sodden turf. It was the last game at Wembley before it was rebuilt and it proved to be an inglorious end. Incongruously there were fireworks at the end of the match and it was impossible to avoid the words 'damp' and 'squib' springing to mind. A section of the crowd was reduced to singing: 'Stand up if you won the War.'

Keegan trooped off looking like a drowned rat, accompanied by boos as he made that walk round the old greyhound track from halfway line to dressing-rooms. Usually he was swift to arrive at press conferences, either keen to placate, to explain reasons for defeat or to bask in victory. Now time dragged on as we waited for him in the medical room that then served as press-conference venue.

It later transpired that he'd been advising his players of his decision to quit.

'It was the old hot, sweaty Wembley dressing-rooms,' says Davies. 'As you go in, it is left for the changing area and right up some steps to the toilets and the plunge baths. As I went in, Tony Adams and David Beckham were shouting at me, "You tell him, David; he'll listen to you."'

'He came in the dressing-room afterwards for a moment then he walked out,' Adams recalls. 'I followed him and we were in an area between the toilets and the baths. He basically said that he didn't think he was good enough. I could see from the look in his eye that he had had enough.

'David Davies tried to talk him out of it. I asked him to reconsider,' adds Adams, who would himself call time on his international career that day. 'We were all saying, "Don't be impulsive, take your time. It's not the end of the world. Think about it." But he was gone. He is an emotional man.'

'It was an impossible scene,' adds Davies. 'The only place to talk was in a toilet cubicle. He said, "I'm going. Let's go and do the press." I said, "If you're going to say that, you are going nowhere. You can't have your employers in the banqueting hall seeing this on TV. I'll get them down here."

'I was playing for time, trying to calm him down. But I knew this was an instinctive guy and it was a forlorn hope. Adam Crozier and Noel White came down but it was over. I don't think Adam ever quite saw Kevin as his coach. That's not to say there was any animosity but I never detected they developed a relationship. I regretted that.

'Kevin took himself back to the team hotel at Burnham Beeches and took his things. When I got back there he was gone.'

That was after his interviews with Sky, the BBC and the written press, during which he poignantly announced with self-lacerating frankness that 'I am just not the man for the job. I have not been quite good enough.'

Indeed, Keegan's record of eighteen games contained only seven wins and he drew another seven, losing four. Steve McClaren would go on to have an even worse record, but at the time Keegan's appeared woeful even in comparison to Graham Taylor's.

Allowing for the criticism that had built up and overcome him during what was clearly an emotional time following the death of his mother, the decision was still out of the blue. There had been no hint of his mood in his programme notes that day. 'I'm not a person who goes into a deep depression after a defeat,' he wrote. 'I try to remain upbeat. I'm realistic enough to know that results are often unpredictable and when all is said and done, things don't always work out as one would wish.' The evidence that Keegan made knee-jerk decisions was growing.

As Adams recognises: 'He wants to be wanted, wants to be loved. He needs to feel that the people are behind him and I think he sensed they weren't. There will always be one or two who don't want you but if seventy-five to eighty per cent are behind you, you can do the job. I think Kevin gets to the stage that if it's fifty–fifty he's walking.

'In Kevin's thinking, "No matter what you can or can't do, if I don't feel loved I will go somewhere where I am wanted."'

Life moved on very quickly. Within hours, FA and international committee vice-chairman David Dein was recommending Sven Goran Eriksson, sensing now that England needed overseas expertise. David Davies's communications with the players before Keegan's appointment had suggested that they might soon be ready to accept a foreign coach; he was soon on the phone with the Swede's agent, Athole Still.

'Kevin's strengths? His work rate, his determination,' says Adams. 'He was a bubbly character. His warmness, his honesty. He is an emotional guy and I admire that. I am very proud that I have had no PR training and I like that about Kevin as well. People like all that "I'd love it, I'd love it" kind of stuff because it comes from the gut. Too many people get the PR treatment and go to interviews with the "Yes sir, no sir". Yes, he risks being hurt because he is open, but people forgive him because of that. People identify with that.'

And Keegan's weaknesses? 'His tactics,' says Adams, now assistant manager of Portsmouth. 'But then I am new to the game of coaching. All I can say is that he has had opportunities to win stuff and hasn't so maybe there are reasons for that.

'Sticking to my experiences as a player, because now as a coach I look at things differently, I don't think he understands the unit, or about balance of personnel, nor rotation of position. But then I compare with Terry Venables and under Kevin we got stuck in formation without fluidity.

'I don't think he got the balance of experience around him. The right staff can complement you, like Sir Alex Ferguson with Carlos Queiroz – the hard-working Scottish side with the technical South American side; one in your face, one more fluid.

'Kevin had Arthur Cox and Derek Fazackerley and I just thought he was missing that top, top experienced European-style coach to guide him. Maybe we should put the last one and the new one together.' Now there would have been a thought; a combination of Glenn Hoddle and Kevin Keegan or Keegan and Sven Goran Eriksson in the job.

Undoubtedly the England job means working in not so much a goldfish bowl as a Damien Hirst tankful of sharks. Keegan himself has described it as 'soulless'. He added: 'The players aren't really yours. They're on loan . . . In my time, it was ridiculous. There was a dearth [of English players]. If you look at clubs then, most had just one, two, maybe three.

'Another element is friendlies. Have a look at those I played as a manager. They were top notch. We never played any knockovers – we played Argentina, France and Brazil. My record is probably the worst but if I swapped my friendlies with easy rides it might have been the best.'

'I think he got frustrated with the gap between games, as international managers often do, particularly if he'd had a duff result,' says Davies. 'But I found him a good person to work with and he became a celebrity coach, well thought of abroad. He always had a welcome for everyone.'

However, Keegan was accurate in his own assessment. The job suited neither his temperament nor his need to be involved on a daily basis. No matter how much passion and pride he brought to it, much of it went to waste when more technical expertise was required. He'd certainly fallen short in the context of international football.

He knew it, and he knew he needed to get back in the saddle with a club side.

10

City Type

The stigma associated with the England job – or, more specifically, with failure in the England job – lingers long and few escape its consequences. It is just one reason why the job is probably best suited to an older man, someone near the end of his career who can not only shrug off its vilification but can also afford not to worry about what he will do afterwards.

In the modern history of the England team Sir Bobby Robson was an exception to this theory. He actually went on to confirm himself as one of the very best after 1990, when his team exceeded expectations at the World Cup in Italy and reached the semi-finals. Before the tournament, however, even during its group stages as England looked unlikely to do well, he was being ridiculed. He knew that the FA were not renewing his contract, so he organised a job with PSV Eindhoven; as was not the case for Don Revie, Robson's employers were fully aware and accepting of his decision.

Robson went on to win a Dutch title, and more honours in Portugal with Sporting Lisbon and in Spain with Barcelona, before he finally accepted the Newcastle job, two years after Keegan's departure, and went on to take them to third, fourth and fifth in the Premiership.

With England after Robson, Graham Taylor's reputation was so damaged that he is still best recalled by the average England fan for failing to qualify for the 1994 World Cup. No matter that he enjoyed a couple of seasons back among friends at Watford, leading them to promotion to the Premiership (then taking them straight back down); no matter, either, that before England he led Watford through all four divisions to third place in the top flight, then took Aston Villa to runners-up.

Terry Venables did enjoy a second wind as a coach after taking England to the semi-finals of Euro '96, but it was transient and unsettled. He took charge of Australia, Portsmouth, Middlesbrough and Leeds before being associated – and doing well to be not too closely associated – with Steve McClaren's flop. McClaren's tenure resembled Keegan's in terms of both duration (eighteen games, over sixteen months) and level of result, yet Keegan's just remained the worst of a full-time appointee to the national team job.

After Venables, Glenn Hoddle struggled at Wolves and Southampton and still licks his wounds. His latest, quite Keeganesque project is the setting up of an academy for young players in Spain; this in preference to the modern ridicule that can now hound those in management. After Keegan, Sven Goran Eriksson still shakes off the lambasting that followed the end of his early promise in the job.

There was considerable debate at Manchester City when Eriksson was appointed to the job there by the former Thai prime minister Thaksin Shinawatra, who had just taken over the club with money accumulated from his homeland. City fans feared the jibes from other supporters, notably Manchester United's, at the hiring, for Eriksson had not made the most of a golden generation of players, having lost a penalty shootout to Portugal in a World Cup quarter-final.

But he came and dispensed with the doubts. In fact his spending of Shinawatra's millions paid off and he took City to the top of the Premier League early on, before he paid the price for a feeble second half of the season and was ruthlessly sacked. This by an owner whose reputation, according to Amnesty International, was for ruthlessness of a more physical nature. Shinawatra duly incurred the wrath of City fans, who were appeased only when Mark Hughes was named as successor. Eriksson took the job of managing Mexico to the 2010 World Cup, while the club changed hands again, with the consortium Abu Dhabi United buying out Shinawatra and promising huge funds, starting with the signing of the Brazilian Robinho for a new British record of £34million.

Quite apart from his much inferior record Keegan would probably not enjoy any comparison with Eriksson. Keegan's teams are, characteristically, about swagger and entertainment; the Swede's sides were well assembled but ultimately lacking in any real inspiration. Except, that is, for the early astonishing and memorable 5–1 win over Germany in

Munich, which repaired England's 2002 World Cup qualifying campaign after Keegan's 1–0 reverse at Wembley.

But Keegan, too, faced some antipathy when in May 2001 he was appointed City manager, having spent six months keeping a low profile after his England departure. The Maine Road support was still based mainly on Moss Side and was unsure about this figure who had been roundly condemned for his record with England. Indeed it's likely that some of them were among those who filled the phone-ins with that assessment of him: according to a phrase often repeated in the manner of cheap verbal currency, Keegan was known to be tactically naïve.

Not that Keegan would have been taking much notice at the time, for when he departs football he departs it properly and takes little interest in the game. Nevertheless as he nursed his grievances following that rainy autumn day at Wembley, Manchester City were embarking on a run of six consecutive Premier League defeats. Under Joe Royle they had just been promoted from Division One as runners-up but were now well out of their depth.

Opening day, and a 4–0 defeat at Charlton, had showed them what they were up against and other big defeats, including 4–1 at home to Charlton, followed as they shipped four goals or more on no fewer than six occasions. They finished in eighteenth position, eight points adrift of safety, and Royle was sacked.

A mess they may have been, and their angst heightened by

United winning another League title, but City will always be attractive to potential managers. Because of a loyal and passionate fan base that may not rival United's for out-of-town volume but does give them an earthy appeal within the city limits, the job can alert the interest of the big names.

This time there was a worthy list of contenders, including David Platt, George Graham, Steve McMahon and Dave Bassett, but it hardly contained the top-drawer name that City fans were hoping for. Keegan was not in the frame; out of sight, out of mind. City were slightly disillusioned now. It was becoming something of a hot potato of a job. In the fifteen years that Sir Alex Ferguson had then been in charge at Old Trafford, City had had nine managers.

But the club now had some shrewd movers and shakers behind the scenes. John Wardle and David Makin were partners in the fast-growing JD Sports chain and the powers behind the throne on which sat chairman David Bernstein. They remembered the catalytic effect that Keegan had had when Newcastle were in the second tier of the English game. They remembered what he went on to achieve after getting Newcastle promoted. Their club was in a similar condition, in need of a lift, and so they made contact. The former City player and colleague of Keegan with England, Dennis Tueart, now a board member, was deputed to begin proceedings.

Keegan was up for a challenge and his three standard requirements would be fulfilled: one, that the club was owned by people with money; two, that those people were willing to invest that money; and three, that he would be well rewarded for all the effort and commitment he would bring to the job.

At the press conference to introduce Keegan, David Bernstein revealed that City had received twenty applications for the job but had had only one target and cited three qualities that the club, for their part, saw in Keegan. First, his outstanding achievements as a League manager, as evidence of which Bernstein duly raised Keegan's record of promotions with Newcastle and Fulham; second, what the chairman described as 'unique man-management and motivational qualities'; and third, something that had, according to Bernstein, been lacking at the club for twenty, even thirty years – 'real style and flair. We used to be renowned for this but over the years, as the club has struggled, it has been dissipated. This is something our fans really understand and will value.'

Once again Keegan had been smart, having learnt from his bitter experience of the financial fall-out from Newcastle. He had talked City into giving him a rare five-year contract.

Bernstein said that Keegan had been easy to negotiate with, to which Keegan replied that he had clearly sold himself too cheaply. 'Such a poor negotiator,' retorted Bernstein ironically.

Keegan talked about the challenge of City – the usual stuff about sleeping giants – and the brief of his situation. 'I'm not saying I didn't enjoy the England job, because I enjoyed every minute of it,' he said. 'But my skills are better suited to club management and working with all parts of the club.' It squared with David Davies's assessment of Keegan's frustrations during his time with England.

And then Keegan let slip that City had first contacted him the night before they sacked Royle. Some were shocked, but it is the way of football: sound out a manager before making your next move.

Keegan immediately appointed Arthur Cox to his scouting staff, though in effect he would again serve as a sounding board; and it would not be long before Derek Fazackerley joined as coach. Royle's assistant, Willie Donachie, remained for a while but decided to take a job with Sheffield Wednesday in the autumn, opening the way for Fazackerley to come from South Yorkshire, having left Barnsley after the sacking of manager Nigel Spackman.

Suddenly, after another of those inspiring initial press conferences, any doubt was overcome. 'There was an excitement,' recalls Gary Owen, the former City and England midfield player who for seven years – including the Keegan era – covered the club as a co-commentator for Century Radio. 'Kevin is very good at putting across his personality and winning people over.'

The season proved to be sensational. City romped to the Division One title, their ninety-nine points being ten clear of West Bromwich Albion, and they scored 108 goals in the process. They won nineteen of their twenty-three home games, losing just one.

It took a while for the side to get going and in October they languished in ninth place, but winning runs of five, six and five games meant a comfortable and joyous end to the season. They scored four goals or more on nine occasions with attacking Keegan football, fluent and overwhelming to the lesser talented, who did not have the same fire power and thus could not test the theory of defensive vulnerability. The acquisition of Stuart Pearce from West Ham, despite him now being thirty-nine, certainly helped in that department.

'I wouldn't say Kevin's tactically naïve by a long chalk,' Pearce has said. 'He loves football to be played a certain way. He wants his teams to go out and try to win games rather than settle for a draw. If you think that's tactically naïve, then that's down to you. But a lot of supporters would say it's a breath of fresh air to play that way.'

The Maine Road support certainly enjoyed it as Keegan brought on the promising teenager Shaun Wright-Phillips and extracted the most out of such eccentric talents as lanky strikers Shaun Goater, who scored twenty-eight goals, and Paolo Wanchope, who netted another twelve.

Coming in from wide, the lightning-quick Darren Huckerby added no fewer than twenty goals and the attacking options did not end there, with the lively Israeli Eyal Berkovic buzzing around just behind the strikers.

Then there was the revelation that was Ali Benarbia. The Algerian had won titles with Monaco, Bordeaux and Paris St Germain, from whom Keegan perceptively recruited him, and at thirty-three he still retained astonishing skills, pulling all the strings from midfield.

Keegan also took on a Colombian conditioning coach called Juan Carlos Osorio, who improved the health and fitness of the squad. All of a sudden there were fewer injuries and all rumours of City being a drinking club went away as Keegan addressed problems with Jeff Whitley and Richard Dunne, forcing them to shape up or face being shipped out.

'He was fortunate in that he was able to keep the squad that was relegated with Joe and add to it by dipping into the transfer market,' says Gary Owen. 'City had the best squad in the division – they were a Premier League side playing in the Championship, really. They also played a brand of football that made them far and away the best team. To be fair, I think a lot of other managers would have got us out of that League.'

This was Keegan in his element again, fresh and enthusiastic and with a new lease of life as he took hold of a depressed club and lifted their spirits as well as his own after England.

The title was clinched with a 5–1 win at Barnsley and Keegan took the opportunity to thank Arthur Cox for his contribution, taking a swipe at the FA in the process.

'That's the same Arthur Cox the FA wouldn't employ because he was over sixty; and then when Sven Goran Eriksson wanted someone of sixty-four, in Tord Grip, they let him do it,' said Keegan. 'But he is a foreigner so I suppose it is harder to knock. It's the most annoying thing the FA did. And it still rankles because I wasn't allowed to take the people I wanted and that was wrong.'

It was a bitter statement – and in fact there were frequent glimpses of a new acidity in Keegan. The England experience had soured him, as it had Graham Taylor notably. While he was ever quotable, knowing what journalists wanted and being able to think in headlines, he was no longer quite the friendly and approachable figure he had been. Often, to their ire, he would keep press men waiting for much of the afternoon after training as he played head tennis or five-a-side.

'He was haunted by his England experience,' one City insider told me. 'He came with too much damage and too much baggage.' This would inform Keegan's time with City in the Premier League, when he was back in a more intense spotlight.

According to the same source, there was an occasion in a following season when City were live on Sky for a Monday-night game at Norwich City. Keegan arrived at the team hotel in a dark mood and on the way to Carrow Road in the coach began to bend the ear of City's head of communications, Paul Tyrrell, ranting about how the media had changed and could no longer be trusted.

Once the coach pulled up outside the ground and the cameras were trained on him as he descended from the bus, Keegan changed. Now he turned on the charm, smiling and signing autographs, ruffling the hair of kids. Two-faced or ultra-professional? Tyrrell would come to use it as an example to young players about how to behave in public even when the private mood may be painful.

That summer of promotion Keegan signalled his intent to muscle in on the more established clubs in the Premiership, as he had done with Newcastle after getting them up, with the signings of such seasoned campaigners as Peter Schmeichel, Nicolas Anelka, Marc Vivien Foe and Sylvain Distin. There was some controversy surrounding Schmeichel, though – not because he was a United legend but because he came from the agent Paul Stretford's Proactive company. Proactive later came to represent Wayne Rooney amid acrimony and a court case involving a previous representative, and Stretford was consequently fined and disciplined by the FA. Keegan held 200,000 shares, then worth £28,000, in the company. It echoed some of Keegan's movements in the market when it came to Stretford clients at Fulham.

There was nothing illegal in Keegan's association with Stretford, however, and it was all overshadowed by the coup of signing Anelka for £13million from Paris St Germain after Liverpool, who had had him on loan for half the previous season, passed on making him a permanent acquisition. Like Benarbia before him, and David Ginola before that, Anelka cited his admiration for Keegan as a former European Player of the Year as one reason for signing. The money, around £40,000 a week – and Keegan persuaded his board to get with the wages being paid now for top talents – would also have helped.

After a poor start, which saw City drop into the bottom three in November, Keegan rallied the troops and they finished a creditable ninth. This was actually below expectation, given the recruiting he had managed and the hype surrounding him. He was forgiven much, though, for a 3–1 win over Man United in which Anelka contributed one of his fourteen goals of the season.

Late the previous season Keegan had paid £5million for the striker Jon Macken from Preston North End, only for him to make just a handful of substitute appearances. Now Keegan collected another striker, Robbie Fowler. To keep him company Steve McManaman arrived from Real Madrid on a free transfer; like Fowler's, his wages were nonetheless high. In addition a young lad by the name of Joey Barton was beginning to make an impression in City's midfield.

It all looked promising as City now left Maine Road for Eastlands, the City of Manchester Stadium that had hosted the 2002 Commonwealth Games and which the council was now leasing to the club. Peter Schmeichel retired and Keegan recruited David Seaman for a last hurrah; remarkably he kept Anelka, so the Frenchman thus spent a rare second season at a club. Tragedy struck that summer, however, when Marc Vivien Foe collapsed and died while playing for Cameroon.

The death cast a shadow over the club and would take some time to lift. City did make a decent start to the season that saw them rise to fifth at the beginning of November but they fell away badly, finishing sixteenth though never in any real relegation trouble. This time Anelka contributed sixteen goals and there were another seven from the fast-improving Shaun Wright-Phillips, who scored twice in a 6–2 win over Bolton. Having qualified for the UEFA Cup via their fair-play record, they went out to Polish side Groclin on away goals in the second round.

'That gap from Championship to Premiership is the biggest leap,' says Gary Owen. 'But it looked as if the team was not going to get where Kevin wanted us to get.'

Nevertheless Keegan was again lauded, and many of his shortcomings overlooked, after another remarkable victory over United, this time by 4–1. There was also an astonishing Cup tie of the sort that only Keegan sides seem to produce. Having trailed 3–0 at half-time at Tottenham in the fourth round of the FA Cup, they somehow won 4–3. All this with ten men after Joey Barton was sent off.

It seems that Keegan was not quite the inspiration many had believed, however. 'It was down to Arthur Cox,' the club insider says. 'He was the guy who pulled the team around at half-time, telling them to play for their pride and dignity. Kevin didn't say much at all.'

Pessimistic City supporters would tell you that a 3–0 lead was once the basis for a draw. Now, under Keegan, it was the basis for a fightback. Equally typically, in the next round, City lost 4–2 to Manchester United.

Keegan's luck began to turn during the following season. Though he had rejuvenated City, with them he had never been able to make quite the same impact on the Premier League as he had with Newcastle, to take the club up a level and into the top tier. Neither was the football quite the entertaining brand associated with Keegan.

'He could play that cavalier approach in the Championship but not in the Premiership in the same way,' says Gary Owen. 'The team wasn't good enough and he didn't have the players. It was a big transition all over.'

Results were reasonable, if unspectacular, as City hovered in mid-table; but friction was growing between Keegan and the board. All at the club were unhappy over an incident at a Christmas party when Joey Barton, after a few drinks, stubbed a cigar on the eyelid of one of the club's younger players, Jamie Tandy. Keegan fined Barton six weeks' wages and the incident blew over.

But the manager was unhappy about treading water and wanted more money for more and better players, as he always did, while his employers began to question some of his signings and what he had done with what he had been given.

Robbie Fowler was often injured and his sporadic goals proved expensive. Steve McManaman's contribution was also fitful. 'Bringing McManaman in looked like good business,' says Owen. 'I saw his first game, against Aston Villa, and he ran the show. After that, he never quite showed the form he did for Liverpool and Real Madrid.'

In addition, David Seaman's appointment had not worked out so David James had to be recruited from West Ham and demonstrated that he was worth the money paid for him. Not so Mikkel Bischoff, who cost £750,000 but made one appearance in four years. The Dane was another Paul Stretford client and the Proactive agency received a fee of £350,000 for their role in the deal.

Meanwhile, David Sommeil cost £3.5million but was also a meagre contributor. Then there was Lucien Mettomo, the Cameroon defender who disappeared in a second season having cost £1.5million, and Christian Neouai, another £1.5million, from Charleroi. On top of the £5million for the forgotten Macken, there was also £3.5million for Vicente Matias Vuoso, an Argentinian striker who never made an appearance.

It was a sale, though, that triggered the beginning of the end for Keegan. In February Anelka departed to the Turkish club Fenerbahce for £7million and in the same month City also went out of the FA Cup to Oldham. The moods of both the manager and the club were shifting.

For Keegan this brochure was also proving fanciful. The club had debts heading north of £60million, Wardle and Makin had advanced £20million of this in loans and were having to consider selling the club (this would eventually let in Shinawatra); Keegan knew that they would have to cash in on their prime asset, Wright-Phillips (in the event Chelsea paid £25million for him in the summer). City had become a selling club and Keegan does not do selling clubs.

'He had spent £52million and said he needed more,' says Gary Owen. 'It should have been enough to get us into a better position. There must have been a budget in operation and I don't think the board was in a position to back him any more. John Wardle went deeper into his personal resources than a lot of chairmen do.'

Keegan was clearly growing frustrated with his side's inability to get close to a Cup or break into the top echelon of clubs. 'We've got a history of not building on good situations,' he said after the team lost to Bolton and slipped to twelfth. 'We could have jumped into the European shake-up but again we couldn't make that leap. That's seven or eight times in a year we could have jumped into something good for this club and we've failed.'

He could be crabby and cranky and this fact clearly rubbed off on people around him. Several players I contacted for their views of their time at City under Keegan were reluctant to talk, unwilling to recall unhappy episodes. One said simply: 'I think I'll pass on that one.' Had he not got on with him? 'You could say that. Let's just say he's an interesting man.'

Keegan was growing disillusioned, too. 'He seemed to be having less and less impact on the team and the fans,' says Owen. 'In the end I don't think he could do any more. I think

Kevin would be the first to say that he lost his enthusiasm. Like a lot of Premier League clubs outside the top four, he ran out of money and a lot of the players had their best years behind them.'

'It was sad towards the end,' the club insider adds. 'His training schedule was weak to say the least. He was giving players two days off in the middle of the week, mainly because he didn't want to be there himself.

'He had had enough. He had been told there was money to spend but the financial situation changed and the reality hit home. Kevin had the prospect of buying players on the cheap and he didn't like that. He wanted to be put out of his misery but John Wardle was too nice and too loyal. It was left to the chief executive, Alistair Mackintosh, to tell him.'

Keegan forced the club's hand by making it clear that he would not be extending his contract, which had another season to run. He probably knew the sort of scrutiny he stood to attract, and that he could be labelled a lame-duck manager; so he was willing to negotiate a pay-off. Come March 2005, with the speculation rife and his position untenable, Keegan departed.

'He never said goodbye to anybody,' says Owen. 'He was just gone and off the face of the earth, like he does, and nobody heard of him again for a while.'

There seemed to be some sense of relief among the players, as well as in Keegan. 'There was a lack of specific goal-setting,' David James told Radio 5 Live. 'I like to know where I'm going – but it would be wrong of me to criticise what's been going on because I've never worked in that side of the profession.'

Stuart Pearce took over as manager and did well. City went eight games unbeaten to the end of the season and it was only a missed Robbie Fowler penalty kick in the last game against Middlesbrough that denied them a place in Europe.

Keegan, meanwhile, was once again weary of the game. His butterfly mind was by now elsewhere, trained on the resurrection of his Soccer Circus project – on which he always seemed to fall back. His affair with management and English football, in the professional sense at least, seemed finally to be at an end. Once more he went into exile, seemingly having fallen out of love with the game.

11

Tyne and Tide

Kevin Keegan has always believed himself to have the spirit of the informed gambler, even the canny businessman. 'I saw myself as an entrepreneurial sort of person who could dream up ideas and get them put into practice,' he said in his autobiography.

In the context of football, playing contracts and, with the help of his former agent Harry Swales, a glut of sponsorship deals, it is true that he has always known how to negotiate well on his own behalf. He has, however, been less successful with certain business ventures he has undertaken off his own bat.

When he first returned to Newcastle as a player, Keegan and fellow horseracing enthusiast Terry McDermott formed a gambling syndicate, but they suffered early heavy losses and the endeavour was quickly abandoned. He had been unfortunate, too, when he decamped to Spain and quit playing football, that the French bootwear company Patrick, who had sponsored him as a player and with whom he had a four-year contract to serve as an ambassador, went bust just one year into that contract. It was meant to pay £250,000 a year to help towards funding his retirement.

Keegan had received some advice about business early in his career, from no less than Bobby Moore. In partnership with James Bond 007 himself, Sean Connery, Moore had been involved in a clothing company and a country club. He told Keegan that the only enterprise from which he'd profited was a sports shop near the West Ham ground. The message was: stick to what you know.

After leaving Manchester City, Keegan went back to what he had known for almost twenty years now: Soccer Circus. It took another year to get it up and running, but finally, in September 2006, he opened what he described as 'the world's first fully interactive football attraction'.

Soccer Circus is located in a hangar-like construction near Glasgow Airport, on a retail park in Braehead (near the run-down area of Govan from where Sir Alex Ferguson hails). It is best described as a giant arcade that features games involving passing, running, dribbling and shooting. As with everything he attempts, Circus ringmaster Keegan – perfectly at ease among the public – threw himself into the project, taking bookings and sessions, even waiting tables, making pizza or serving drinks in the bar that he had named Shankly's.

Keegan had certainly been wary of the media since coming to the conclusion that many journalists have made him a victim of his own honesty. All the same, six months in and clearly in need of some publicity for the venture, he agreed to give some interviews. 'This idea has been with me since I retired from playing,' he told Jamie Jackson of the *Observer*. 'It's more important than managing another football club.

'People come in here and ask me all the time about the Alex Ferguson one,' he added of a former life. 'They would say, "I would love it if I beat you round here, just love it." I laugh about it. It certainly doesn't annoy me. I think it's very funny. And a lot of people come up and say, "I really liked your interview, it showed you cared." If you can't laugh at yourself, you can't laugh at anyone.'

His tone seemed to be one of disillusionment and perhaps cynicism, however, when he told Brian Viner of the *Independent*: 'I just see football for what it is, which is all about money. I find it incredible that a doctor can train for eight years to earn in a year half of what a footballer earns in a month.' He could not see himself returning to football management, he added, and had watched barely any games – just a couple in the World Cup finals in the summer of 2006, and not one live Premier League match in the three years since he left Manchester City.

But Soccer Circus struggled. Start-up costs were reported to be up to £6million; and, while he received a grant of £500,000 from the Scottish Executive, who were keen to encourage participation in such a project given the health issues of Glasgow youngsters, Keegan had to sink around £2.4million of his own money into the project – 'almost everything we have got, me and my family', he said. In its first year the venture lost around £1million to April 2007 and Keegan took on an investor, Scottish entrepreneur Peter Barr. Barr's £600,000 investment diminished Keegan's ownership to less than sixty per cent. Keegan was, therefore, ripe for a cash injection.

Harry Redknapp turned down the Newcastle job, prompting shock on Tyneside and criticism of his lack of ambition. Both ignored the realistic view of the club from outside, and stemmed from the unrealistic perception of the club's status and stature as seen within the club and its support.

As Sir Bobby Robson reveals: 'After Kevin resigned in 1997, they came to Barcelona to try and get me. Freddy Shepherd, Freddie Fletcher and Douglas Hall sat in my house in Sitges and tried to persuade me to go. I was very tempted but I was at Barcelona. I had waited sixty years to get there, I had a two-year contract and I was loving it. I had a good team – Ronaldo, Guardiola, Stoichkov, Popescu, Sergi, Abelardo, Nadal, Figo on the right. A good team.

'Freddy Shepherd thought I should just say "bye bye" and sign for Newcastle. They put figures down but I was earning more than they were offering me. They have this innate power over people. They think that because they are Newcastle United everybody should give in.'

Keegan did give in, quite quickly, when Newcastle came for him with the promise that money this time was no issue. Though his return to Tyneside came as something of a shock in other respects, financially speaking there was nothing surprising in his acceptance of a three-and-a-half-year contract that would bring him more than £10million. Not to put too fine a point on it, he needed the job and the money; this time around, given his belief that his previous efforts had made rich men richer, he was going to get his worth.

He knew that he was in a strong position, after all. The club's new owner, Mike Ashley, needed to pull off a coup. After Sam Allardyce and the failure to deliver Redknapp, the fans were growing restless and the chairman appeared to be the butt of their ire. Chairmen will tolerate pressure on managers but not on themselves. When such pressure is felt, they act – often precipitately. Ashley, who loves being popular, went for the popular choice and Keegan saw salvation.

'Would I have gone back under the old regime?' he asked rhetorically at one of his early Friday press conferences, with emerging resentment about how it had ended eleven years previously. 'No, but that doesn't mean to say I don't respect them. If you talk about the way it finished, then it was disappointing. Sir John Hall couldn't even be bothered to come back and say goodbye to me.

'But I understand all those things. I've seen Sir John since and said hello to him. I wouldn't probably go out for dinner with him and Freddy [Fletcher] but you must not cloud that with the fact that I don't respect them, because I do. Douglas Hall is another I respect. He drove this club forward and so much wanted success; and I liked that part of him. But there were other parts, like with everybody you don't like.'

Sir Bobby Robson recalls the day that Keegan's appointment was announced – Wednesday 16 January 2008. Newcastle were to take on Stoke City in their FA Cup third-round replay that night. The third coming was as vibrant as the first two.

'The city was alight, aflame,' says Sir Bob. 'They had sold 25,000 tickets but within two hours that was 44,000. He had put nearly 20,000 on the gate in two hours. I couldn't believe the queues. I was among it. They thought the messiah had returned. It was the most sensational day. That one guy could capture the city with delight and pleasure and excitement.

'Kevin showed up after the game had started and there was this guy sat two seats in front of me who sat watching him all night. He was entranced by him. Never saw the game.' Keegan had no involvement in the game but all concerned thought the magic was rubbing off already as Newcastle won 4–1.

Keegan made all the right noises about Ashley, who would soon be sporting a replica shirt with 'King Kev' on the back. 'I've never met anyone like Mike,' he said. 'He's definitely different but I really like him. He's very unassuming, he's got no ego, he's incredible. If we get this place going, we will have the best owner in this country. I say that: the best. That's what he'll be. But it's an "if" until we get it going.

'He's given us a lot of responsibility now and we've got to make sure we encourage him to stay in this for the real long haul. If we're successful, he will and we don't want to do anything that makes him despondent.' Keegan could almost have been talking about himself there.

And, once again, he endeared himself to the Geordie public and the media alike with an apposite, populist, soundbite about the fans on the day after he took over. The box office now declared: 'Emotion, excitement, passion – free with every seat.'

'They would like to win something, but when they've worked all week they come here to be entertained,' said Keegan. 'It's like the people down South going to a theatre. Newcastle fans want to come to this ground and see something worth seeing. They want to enjoy it. What they don't want is for us to go out, play drably, win 1–0 and maybe finish halfway up the table. They want us to have a go and that's why I'm here.'

Not everyone was so upbeat. Sir Alex Ferguson, in curmudgeonly mood, wondered how it would all pan out. 'Sometimes it is wrong to go back to a club for a second spell,' he said. 'There are examples of managers doing it and having relative success but no outstanding success, so I will be interested to see how Kevin copes with it . . . As soon as that phone went, a part of him must have thought, "Oh, there's unfinished business here." It's excitement and we all need that in our life.'

Privately, some other managers may have questioned it. One manager told me that he felt Keegan's return was an insult to the profession, that it sent out the wrong message – if a man who had been out of touch with the game could walk back into a top job, football management must be a pretty easy occupation.

That apart, amid such a prevailing upbeat mood on Tyneside, Keegan was thus granted more indulgence than any other manager might have been as results continued to worry with winter turning to spring. The optimism gave way to realism as the so-called credit crunch began to affect Ashley's business affairs, a fact that seriously restricted Keegan's ability to do business and that gradually led to internal strife. The exciting opening night and all the fine words became buried amid anxiety and conflict.

All groups of fans believe that the affairs of their club would make a soap opera. Newcastle has always had elements of such. This one starred Mike Ashley as Phil Mitchell and Kevin Keegan mutating from the feisty Mike Baldwin into the acquiescent Ken Barlow.

To mix the characters further, we almost had Alan Shearer – once described by Freddy Shepherd as the Mary Poppins of football – playing Mini Me. For Newcastle supporters were being teased by what many saw as the dream ticket of Shearer's possible return to the club to work with Keegan as his second-in-command.

Old wounds were reopened when we were reminded that the pair had not spoken for eighteen months. Shearer was apparently miffed by Keegan's decision to remain on a family holiday in the USA rather than attend Shearer's testimonial at St James'.

'It is possibly true that it did offend him in some way,' Keegan admitted. 'Things like that sadly may have affected him. But it hasn't affected me and I want to talk to him.'

The pair did talk but could not reach agreement; the dynamic was unworkable. Keegan needed to be in sole charge while Shearer would see himself as a number one, would want to stand or fall by his own decisions rather than by someone else's. The timing was wrong. He remained in his job with BBC television.

And so Keegan soldiered on. To follow that Manchester United 5–1 home debacle came a 1–0 defeat by Blackburn Rovers at St James'. The game was lost with almost the last kick of the game and in almost pure Keegan fashion as Newcastle, desperate to win, threw men forward at a corner, allowing Matt Derbyshire to break for a winner courtesy of an open back door. A point would have been welcome for Newcastle to stop some rot but the chance was missed, as if a goalless draw was beneath a Keegan side. It illustrated not so much a flaw of ambition, however, as an oversight of detail, with the openness at the back ignored.

Keegan was forced to defend himself and his methods, insisting that his absence from the game was not the cause of Newcastle's problems. 'There is no lack of knowledge and I have tremendous knowledge around me as well,' he maintained. He may well have been referring to Terry McDermott, who had acquired a new nickname from Keegan of Black Box for his having survived all the managers who succeeded Keegan over the past decade. Arthur Cox, now sixty-nine, had also returned in an 'advisory capacity' while a former player, Robbie Elliott, joined the coaching staff.

Otherwise, Keegan cleared out some of Allardyce's copious technical-support staff – twenty-five of them involved in medical, fitness, scouting and videoing capacities, it was reported – while retaining others, including Steve Round, the well-respected coach who had worked with Steve McClaren at Middlesbrough and England. Until Round decamped to work with David Moyes at Everton, that was.

'It's a work in progress,' Keegan said. 'It does not always happen straight away but takes a few weeks, a few matches. We need to win a football match to stop everyone saying, "You haven't won a match since you came here." That's fair comment because we haven't. The stick doesn't bother me but it does bother me that we haven't won a match.

'I wouldn't say I have galvanised the club but we have come in and changed a few things, and I think we will get our rewards for those changes. We are more or less firefighting at the moment as opposed to developing. We are trying to put something right and then move to stage two. Sometimes there is no quick fix. We have to take the cynicism on the chin. We have our destiny in our hands.

'I'm a little bit older, a bit wiser, but I'm the same person. I think I have the same enthusiasm, although I'm not shouting from the rooftops like I did last time because this is not the time to do that. We are in stage one of a redevelopment.'

McDermott defended Keegan on the usual counts. 'People ask, "Will he leave? Is he going to walk out?"' McDermott said. 'There is absolutely no chance. He thinks too much about this club to do that. He has signed a three-and-a-half-year contract and I would be shocked if Kevin was not here for the whole of that.

'He is an emotional personality. He cares about the club very deeply and it hurts him when players and the club get criticised. He wears his heart on his sleeve and does get emotional about certain things but that is his character and you are not going to change that.'

Through the chairman, Chris Mort, on secondment from Ashley's lawyers Freshfields to oversee the day-to-day running of the club, Newcastle issued statements of support for Keegan; but privately they grew worried. Ashley spoke to Keegan about the spectre of relegation. Keegan said he thought they would stay up but could not guarantee it.

Off the field began the mutterings and mumblings and there emerged a curious hierarchy at St James' Park that told of already existent cracks and creaks within the club.

Ashley's great friend and former business partner Paul Kemsley had not long resigned as Tottenham Hotspur vice-chairman, ostensibly to concentrate on his business affairs. This did not preclude him offering Ashley his help and advice. One such suggestion was to employ the services of a

London-based property developer and supposed football Mr Fix-It, Tony Jimenez, who had helped to bring Juande Ramos to Spurs from Seville as replacement for Martin Jol.

Between them, Jimenez and Kemsley persuaded Ashley to hire their friend Dennis Wise as a director in charge of football, for a salary of £1.5million. Wise quit his position as Leeds United manager to take up the post. Bizarrely, it later emerged, Jimenez had first got to know Wise when he was a senior steward at Chelsea – a great example of a man rising without trace.

Football was shocked. Wise scarcely seemed qualified, given the wealth of experienced senior figures capable of scouting and recruiting players from around Europe. Even more shocked was Kevin Keegan, who had been told that the club were to appoint such a figure – someone who would be given the job title of executive director (football) – but had had no say in that person being Wise. To add to the potion, a 'technical co-ordinator' said to have good knowledge of the European game arrived in the shape of Jeff Vetere, an Englishman who had once been a youth-academy coach at Rushden and Diamonds and who had latterly spent four months at Real Madrid.

Everyone feared the moment when Keegan would declare that it was not like the brochure, but he kept his counsel. For now. Perhaps he was pacified when he was consulted on the proposed recruitment of Chris Hughton, who had left Tottenham when Jol was sacked, as his new assistant – a recruitment to which Keegan agreed.

While he was undoubtedly perturbed by the way the club was structured and run, he perhaps also realised that now was not a time to fight battles. It was certainly not a time to cut and run. All the same, this was far from being the attractive new regime he'd expected it to be; with most of the club's hierarchy being based in the South it began to feel a bit like the last days of his previous reign, when he could rarely get hold of board members who were otherwise engaged.

Wise was assigned an office in the North-East but it was at the youth academy at the Little Benton site rather than at the main Long Benton training ground half a mile away. Though the two might have been expected to have been in frequent contact, Keegan described the arrangement as 'for the best'.

Results worsened. An embarrassed Keegan had to endure taunts from the Kop that once adored him as Newcastle lost 3–0 at Anfield. That Saturday afternoon, Wise was spotted with his family at *The Lion King* musical in London's West End. He was supposed to be roaming Europe looking for players – Keegan had asked Ashley what he was doing in directors' boxes watching the games and Ashley, reportedly, suggested to Wise that he might be best off absenting himself from Keegan's sight for a while.

That sight had lost its twinkle. During interviews Keegan looked tired and weary, the bags under the eyes saggier. That assessment quoted in Chapter 1 in the *Daily Telegraph* by Graham Taylor continued: 'Has he been totally responsible for the new incoming staff members or have they been imposed on him? Does he really mean it when he says he is happy with the attitude and approach of the players at his disposal? Does he really believe that a couple of wins will give his players the confidence to shoot up the table?

'Like it or not, the Kevin Keegan I know – or thought I knew – gave it to you straight, both verbally and eyeball to eyeball. That was a major part of his appeal. It seems that is now not the case. I'm worried.'

On the Monday after the Liverpool defeat a rumour spread through Tyneside: Keegan was to be sacked; Terry Venables was to take over with Dennis Wise as his sidekick. The rumour was swiftly denied but was symptomatic of the frenzied atmosphere that was developing.

Factions emerged, with different sections of the club preferring to use different media outlets in their attempts to clarify and solidify their positions. It was revealed, for example, that Keegan had presented Ashley with a wish-list of players that included Ronaldinho and David Beckham. This had an element of truth – Keegan's penchant for big names who could excite the public being no secret – but the report also said that Ashley was not into short-term stardust.

As they usually do, results put all the intrigue on hold. A point at Birmingham City helped before Newcastle finally, after ten games and sixty-four days with Keegan in charge, beat Fulham 2–0 at St James'. Keegan's side had gone into the game just three points clear of the drop zone with eight games to go. There was huge relief all round.

'Forget me,' said Keegan. 'It's important for the club, the players and our magnificent supporters.' He hadn't taken wife Jean out for a while, he said, and would be doing so that night.

Now Newcastle had a bit of confidence and won exceptionally well, in old-Keegan fashion, by 4–1 at Tottenham then 3–0 at home to Reading. Keegan looked better.

Mark Lawrenson, once Keegan's defensive coach at Newcastle, noted that: 'When he took over, they weren't winning and he looked tired, a bit hangdog. They start winning and the lines were gone. You can always tell with Kevin, that's the way he is. He walks in looking at his feet and you think, "What's wrong with the gaffer? He's not happy today." It's not like it can be gone in a minute. He's the kind of person who can be gone.'

'He restored some bubble and some sparkle to the team,' adds Sir Bobby Robson. 'The bite and the enthusiasm and the spirit was there compared to the beginning of the season. I saw a better face on the players than under Sam.'

Now Newcastle were all but safe and Keegan even sounded better. A goalless draw at Portsmouth was the product of a dull, lifeless game but he was in relaxed and talkative mood. He lauded Michael Owen to the skies, having found a new role for him playing deeper behind Mark Viduka and Obafemi Martins. It was to give Owen space and an opportunity to use his maturing football brain, said Keegan. The new England manager, Fabio Capello, should consider him in the role.

Portsmouth assistant Tony Adams has another explanation, based on his experiences of playing for England under Keegan. 'I'm not sure he could make a decision about who to drop,' he says. '"If I drop this player, do I get a result?" I don't think he has done that in his thinking.'

Keegan's assessment of Owen was manna to football reporters who needed something to liven up a dull report. There was a subtext to Keegan's words, too. This was clearly part of a message to Mike Ashley: fork out to keep the star striker at the club with a deal to replace the one that was running down. Owen was on £6million a year, which was a bit rich for Ashley's tastes.

It was, too, part of a bridge-building process. Keegan would need Owen's goals, would make him captain, but he needed to dispel any lingering resentment the player may have felt as a result of his England experiences under Keegan.

'I assume the manager had conveyed to his staff what he thought of me and plainly it wasn't complimentary,' Owen had said in his autobiography. 'I felt I was being singled out . . . There was so much pressure on him he needed a scapegoat – as soon as he said one negative thing about me, it led to another one and then it became a habit.

'Looking back on the Keegan era, one main feature stands out for me. It made me question my footballing ability for the first time in my life. And yes, it scarred me. I used to go into games believing the opposition was scared of me and that nothing could get in my way. That feeling, that belief, evaporated at times when I played under Keegan. Certainly it was a dark phase in my career. It made me more sensitive and self-protective.'

Another victory – and a major one in terms of atmosphere on Tyneside – by 2–0 over Sunderland, saw Newcastle now having gone six matches unbeaten. This certainly helped loosen Keegan's tongue and brought to light some of the simmering issues at the club.

Keegan made it clear that he, not Wise or Jimenez, would be signing players. 'Dennis and Tony are not there to say, "We've got to sign this player,"' he said. 'They're there to say, "You should go and look at this player" – and that's how it's working.

'They've already put names forward, but until we see them they won't come into this football club. If we think like Dennis and Tony do when we see them, we'd love to have them at Newcastle. If they bring players in and they're not my players, I wouldn't be managing this football club.' Keegan was still seeking stardust, and was linked with a £15million signing of Thierry Henry from Barcelona.

Then, after defeats by West Ham and Chelsea, before ending the season with a third on the spin at Everton, Keegan increased the pressure on the club's owner.

Having lost 2–0 to Chelsea at St James', Keegan entered the press room, loosened his tie and aimed both barrels of his scattergun, pigeons flying everywhere. The Premier League was the first target as he launched a debate about the state of the game in this country, but the real point of his tirade soon became apparent.

Keegan described the League as 'the most boring great League in the world'. He went on to say that it was all but impossible to repeat this time what he had done with Newcastle last time; he couldn't gatecrash the English game's elite. Chelsea, going for the title that Manchester United ultimately secured, had illustrated to Keegan how far his club were behind.

When he took the job Keegan had described Ashley as the perfect owner because of his passion for the club. Now Keegan said he had a perfect relationship with the owner because the pair never communicated.

'We're a million miles away from challenging for the League but if my owner backs me – and I have no proof of that but no doubt he will – we want to try to finish fifth and top of the other mini-league. I get on great with the owner because I never talk to him.

'The gulf is too big and it certainly will be during my time here,' he said. 'We're the fifth-biggest club in the country in terms of fans and turnover and we can't get in there.

'Even if someone gives you a barrel-load of money, you're not going to get the best. If a player had a choice between Chelsea and Newcastle, you would slaughter him for coming here and not playing in the Champions League. The best players will go to a Champions League club and if they don't make it they will go to Newcastle.'

His words were resonant of the general impression he'd given in his last days at Manchester City: they revealed his frustration in being no longer a major player in the management game.

'I'm not going there,' he said. 'But I felt like this before I got back into the game and being back just underlines it. It's no longer a division where you can be promoted and hope to challenge.

'You have West Brom and Stoke coming up and none of these managers is going to say what I said, "Watch out, Alex, I'm after your title." If they do, people will think they've been on the drink.'

Honest? Realistic? Ashley didn't think so and resented Keegan's defeatism and sideswipes along with the implication that he needed plenty of money if the club were to contemplate the top four.

Keegan's outburst also ignored some facts. In the decade since he left the club, Chelsea had topped the Premier League's transfer spending with £475million, followed by Manchester United with £298million. Liverpool had forked out £264million and in fourth place with £231million was . . . Newcastle. Arsenal had proved that success could still arrive without similar fortunes, having paid out £184million in fees, with their wages also below those of Newcastle.

It could be the way with Keegan. Powerful and superficially convincing as his emotional arguments may be, they struggle sometimes to stand up alongside the facts.

And what he didn't say, what was really bugging him, was that he had missed out on signing the creative midfield player that the side really needed. The little Croat Luka Modric, who would go on to impress at Euro 2008, had that weekend opted to join Tottenham Hotspur for £15.5million from Dinamo Zagreb.

The next day, Chris Mort talked about the club refusing to 'do a Leeds' and extend themselves in the pursuit of glory, only to crash and burn. The day after, it emerged that Keegan had been summoned to a meeting in London at the headquarters of Mort's company Freshfields, for a meeting with Ashley.

During the course of a four-hour showdown attended by Ashley, Keegan, Mort, the new vice-chairman, Derek Llambias (another London-based friend of Ashley, who had run a casino he patronised), Wise and Jimenez, transfer strategy was discussed. Keegan talked about signing proven Premier League players like Wayne Bridge and Shaun Wright-Phillips, both of whom might be prised out of Chelsea.

Wise and Jimenez favoured younger players from overseas who would come cheaper and grow in value. This was in line with Ashley's growing conviction that the club needed to trim its sails, with there being reports that he had discovered around £80million more of debt at the club than he had budgeted for and had had to guarantee around £60million of his own fortune to keep the banks onside.

Keegan was no longer dealing with men like Sir John Hall, Mohamed Fayed and David Bernstein, who were star-struck and revered him. And, much as Ashley so wanted to be popular on Tyneside, he was not about to be dictated to. His history in business told of ruthlessness.

Once, for example, he had spoken to competition watchdogs about rival sportswear boss Dave Whelan, owner of Wigan Athletic, and the rigging of replica-shirt prices. A former chairman of Ashley's Sports Direct company, David Richardson, who crossed Ashley, lasted just three months after the company's stock-market flotation, which brought Ashley personally almost £1billion.

Against that, Ashley rewarded loyalty. After the flotation, five of his long-serving directors shared £25million in bonuses. Knowledge of that would have been of interest to the modern Keegan.

In the end, both parties agreed to bite the bullet and their tongues and show a united front. But Keegan was left in no doubt about who was running the club these days.

That much was also seen from the fact that Mohammed had to come to the mountain. Keegan could have stayed in Newcastle and Ashley could have met him there, since both men were attending a cancer-charity dinner organised by Sir Bobby Robson that night. But Ashley wanted to send the message that he was in charge.

After the meeting Keegan drove back to the North-East through the Friday traffic. Ashley took a private helicopter.

Once upon a time, Keegan would not have tolerated all this, would have expected his owner and board to back him and massage his ego. Now, in this May of 2008, it was clear that, while he was not going to be sacked, as that would have Tyneside in uproar again, he could not expect to get his own way. And, because of his personal circumstances, he had to accept his lot.

'Kevin was always the main spokesman for the club,' says Sir Bobby. 'He always said what he feels and thinks, doesn't hold anything back. He had that power ten years ago but, because he was so popular as a player and a manager, everybody listened and wrote what he said. He was very influential.

'He had come back to a different club. Freddy Shepherd and Freddie Fletcher relied on him, went to him, spoke to him, gave him what he wanted. But it was a different situation now.'

If Newcastle's fans got the impression that all was now well, that owner and manager – whose relationship is pivotal in any football club – had settled any differences and that the summer would see full-scale recruitment and a tilt at the Premier League's bigger clubs, they were mistaken.

It was, in reality, an uneasy truce and this would be far from a summer of love.

12

And Now . . .

If you believe that there's a bond between our future and our past,
Try to hold on to what we have,
We build them strong, we build to last.
'Cause this is a mighty town,
Built upon solid ground,
And everything they've tried so hard to kill,
We will rebuild.

This is a big river,
I want you all to know I'm so very proud,
This is a big river,
But that was long ago,
That's not now.
This is a big, big river,
And in my heart I know it will rise again.
The river will rise again.

'BIG RIVER', JIMMY NAIL

There is no getting away from it: the perception of Kevin Keegan is that he is a mentally fragile character who needs a lot of loving by fans and power-brokers and that if he doesn't get that love, or as soon as the going gets tough, he will simply walk away.

Not that this perception is entirely true or fair. It is incontrovertible that everywhere he has been he has thought about quitting, voiced his musings about moving on in those depressed moments when football gives you a kicking, but is that actually any different from most in their daily lives and jobs? In bouts of soul-searching all of us surely have doubts about what we do, so consider the possibility of doing something else.

The difference in football is that, in this modern media age, openly expressing concerns leads to one's every word being dissected instantly and in many outlets in press and on radio and television, from websites and their message boards to phone-ins. Being more quotable than most, more willing to open up, has put Keegan in the firing line of spontaneous judgement and this can often be less than flattering. Consideration of his record shows that he can stick around if he feels it is worth it. As a player, Keegan stayed for almost four years at Scunthorpe, six at Liverpool. Then came three at Hamburg and two each at Southampton and Newcastle. It is hardly Nicolas Anelka. Later, as a manager, Keegan had five years at Newcastle and almost four at Manchester City. They are almost lifetimes in the stressful and transitory world of football management these days, Sir Alex Ferguson and Arsene Wenger apart. Those two spans made Keegan the longest-serving postwar Newcastle manager after Joe Harvey, and the longest-serving at Manchester City since Tony Book in the seventies.

In between, there were spells of only eighteen months each at Fulham and with England, equal with Steve McClaren as the shortest tenure of a full-time appointee with the national team. His time in one of these jobs, though, was interrupted when his country came calling; the other ended when he felt that he was no longer up to scratch.

It's with that England experience, however, that he is still primarily associated in the eyes of many. And those many usually fall into one of two categories.

There are those who believe that he was brave and honest in owning up to his limitations. Then come those who see him as a quitter. And that is not just public opinion. Professionals wonder, too. Almost everyone I spoke to in the course of writing this book talked about if or when it might end at Newcastle – probably in tears – with him either being sacked for speaking out of turn or deciding to walk out.

Keegan himself says that what he most gets asked about these days is his first management spell at Newcastle, when he and his team captured the imagination of the footballing public and beyond, coming up to the Premier League and taking it by storm, so nearly winning it with an assembly of creative talents and a brand of attacking football that so excited.

Somewhere in among that Newcastle nostalgia and the England experience lies the reality of Keegan and his own attitudes.

On the one hand, his brand of honesty and romanticism about the game is deeply attractive to supporters and television watchers who want simply to enjoy a spectacle that will lift their spirits, especially those for whom times are hard and escapism is a key factor.

On the other, professionals see a flawed approach that will crumble under pressure and never win the games or trophies that could and should be won when such money and resources are at his disposal.

This is just one of the contradictions that are so evident in Keegan. He can be selfish but expansive; generous but on occasion mean of spirit; unconcerned about money but desperate for the best personal deal; he retains loyal friends but has also been known to ditch people who are seemingly no longer useful to him. Keegan loves the game but at times hates its peripheral issues. Where you find him all depends on his mood at the time, and at which point in his career you're looking.

And this is the baggage that Keegan brought with him back to Newcastle.

There may have been more technically adept candidates for the Newcastle job, with men like Mark Hughes, Didier Deschamps and Gerard Houllier being mentioned high on bookmakers' lists, but when Mike Ashley and his cohorts needed quick salvation and solution, Keegan proved to be the most attractive option.

For Keegan, meanwhile, this was an opportunity to have another crack at management, his unfinished business, in the spotlight that is to him a mixed blessing – for it simultaneously feeds his ego and drains his energy and optimism. And, of course, the money helped. The £64million question became, in the financial parlance of the modern Premier League, just how long this marriage of mutual convenience would last.

Once the heat had died down on Newcastle United's unsatisfactory end to the season, and with a momentarily less intrusive glare on their activities, Mike Ashley made some moves.

Chris Mort returned to his law firm and Derek Llambias took over as chairman. Ashley let it be known that he was unhappy with the sums some of the players were earning. There was a curious rumour concerning Sir Alex Ferguson's interest in buying Michael Owen (probably wishful thinking on the part of Owen's advisers), but that notwithstanding Ashley knew that there would now be few, if any, big takers for him; thus he could afford to strike a hard bargain on any new contract.

Ashley and his lieutenants at the club also sought to downgrade the £65,000-a-week contract of midfield player Joey Barton but were thwarted in what also became a test of Keegan's management and authority.

Barton, bought from Manchester City by Sam Allardyce for £5.8million, had a troubled history. After that incident with apprentice Jamie Tandy under Keegan at City, Barton had later also attacked team-mate Ousmane Dabo at the club's Carrington training ground. On top of that, while a Newcastle player, he had been charged with assault for a violent incident in Liverpool city centre over Christmas.

He pleaded guilty in the Dabo case and received a four-month suspended sentence. He was also found guilty of the second assault and was sentenced to six months' imprisonment. Of this he served seventy-four days and was back for pre-season training.

Two days before Barton was released, Keegan went on to the Radio 5 Live show *Sportsweek* – being hosted by his former FA colleague David Davies – and announced that he was willing to give Barton another chance, as he had done at City. Barton could be a contender for a first-team place.

'I told him that, as long as from now on he did things right and started to rebuild the confidence of the people around him, I would stick by him,' said Keegan.

Tyneside was not best pleased, judging by the reaction of fans. They had not liked it the previous season when Barton defended Allardyce and berated them for their lukewarm support and vociferous criticism of players. Now they did not like the idea of a convicted criminal in their side. Keegan had once turned the atmosphere when he sold Andy Cole. It would be interesting to see if he could carry the crowd with him this time or had misjudged the mood. The city had changed; had the support?

Ashley seemed unimpressed as well but he was coming to see the pragmatism of the game known by Keegan, who realised that Newcastle were not so flush with players or money that they could afford to sack Barton. Newcastle had been trying to unload Barton; Bolton Wanderers had shown some interest, but ultimately this came to nothing. The reality was that if they sacked him they'd be giving him a free transfer. Neither could they legally cut his wages, although they had docked them for his time in jail. Keegan's way had prevailed for the moment.

Ashley was not the first owner to be surprised and disgusted at the working practices and conditions of Premier League footballers. Soon he was issuing an edict that the players would have to buy their own club suits for the forthcoming season. It was not the cost of around £20,000 he objected to, apparently, it was just that he wanted to send a message about the gravy train slowing down. Ashley also ordered an internal assessment of players' car expenses and mobile-phone bills.

'Mike wants to make a point,' a club source was quoted as saying. 'He's fed up with seeing guys on eighty grand a week doing nothing and lying on the treatment table all the time. Yes, he's trying to cut costs and is looking at every department but he also wants to take some players down a peg or two. He has a real bee in his bonnet about this.'

Ashley also consented to basic season-ticket prices rising by ten per cent, at a time when inflation was around four per cent, the average hike in the Premier League was seven per cent and the credit crunch was biting. Prices would be frozen, however, for supporters who bought for three years – which begged the question of what might happen in years two and three without any increased income.

There was a time when Keegan would have been party to all these decisions, would have been consulted by a board who valued his input and took his advice. He was, after all, once the catalyst of the club, the fulcrum who made it all work both on and off the pitch. Now, increasingly, the impression being given was that he was 'merely' a manager, who should get on with putting a team out on the field with what he was given and should let the big boys get on with the important stuff behind the scenes.

It recalled a moment from the BBC political-comedy series *The Thick of It* when chief government enforcer and spin-doctor

Malcolm Tucker, the Alastair Campbell figure played by Peter Capaldi, was asked teasingly why he was not in the loop. Tucker replied, 'Not in the loop? Not in the loop? I *am* the fucking loop.' Keegan had in the past been the be-all and end-all of the decision-making process. Now, it seemed, he was simply informed of the decisions that had been made.

Times had changed for Keegan. He took his first exile in Spain, for seven years, yet came back and got quickly up to speed – no matter how astronomical the prices for players then were and how little he knew about the current crop of talent. He had energy and enthusiasm, would take off at the drop of a hat to see matches, absorbing information quickly and relying on his often-correct gut instincts.

Mark Lawrenson, then one of Keegan's coaches, tells of the club being in the UEFA Cup and drawn against the French club Metz. One morning before training, Lawrenson recalls: 'He said, "They've got a match tonight so we'll go and watch them." I said it would take a while to get there. He said, "Don't worry about it, we've got a private plane and we'll go after training."'

It was clear in the first few interviews he gave after his three-year exile post-Manchester City that Keegan was now more realistic, more condemnatory about the nature of the game. His views on the Premier League should have been obvious during those conversations, too, but no one picked up on them, perhaps because he was perceived as a yesterday's man rather than as the manager of one of the country's leading clubs.

The story goes, so one person in television told me, that Keegan gave an interview at his Soccer Circus in Glasgow to Gabby Logan for BBC 1's *Inside Sport*. At the end of the interview the producer thanked him for keeping the venue closed while they filmed. Keegan replied that it had not been closed, that it was business as usual. The emptiness of the place offered an insight into why he was ready to return to football management.

In his absence the game had also changed. His had always been an intuitive approach to management, his selections based on hunches, his tactics based on his feel for his players, the game that day and the opposition. Now it was clear that a more scientific approach to the sport was the norm – though perhaps not to the extent of the twenty-five support staff whom Allardyce had hired. Like Keegan, Arsene Wenger may be a romantic in his ideas about the way the game should be played, but he has always been a pioneer of strict training methods and a rigorous regime. As Tony Adams noted of his time with England, this was a very different attitude to Keegan's.

On the contrary, it would seem that Keegan has always mistrusted the coaches. 'I had done all my coaching badges early on,' says Fulham's Alan Smith. 'I had to get qualified because I knew I wasn't going to get on with my playing record. You could almost see him taking the mick out of that. He didn't really believe in coaching.'

Talk of coaching, Smith adds, got Keegan on to Charles Hughes, the FA's director of coaching when he was playing for England. There were plenty of pictures of Keegan in Hughes's book on tactics and teamwork and apparently Keegan resented the fact that he never got paid for his part in it.

This in turn prompts the memory of how Keegan could on occasion display resentfulness about not making the money he felt he should, and could also be financially demanding. 'I asked him to open officially another bit of a gym we had been using as a youth team,' Smith recalls. 'He said he wouldn't do it for less than £7,000. As a professional I can understand where he was coming from but, as Fulham, we had already been using it.'

Rogan Taylor, Liverpool fan and academic, goes further, describing Keegan as 'an awkward arse because he was a money head'. Taylor was making six one-hour documentaries for the BBC for a series entitled *Kicking and Screaming*, a cultural history of the English game.

'We had identified him as a key and pivotal figure from the modern to the postmodern, a harbinger of things to come,' says Taylor. 'We filmed 356 interviews but we couldn't get him. Well, we didn't pay, did we? I think if we had waved a big enough cheque we would have got him.'

Against that, there have been times when Keegan has gone above and beyond the call of duty in granting interviews and giving of himself. Alan Smith at Fulham noted that Keegan sometimes had to take a couple of days off because he was simply drained. One assumes that these things depended largely on his mood and energy levels.

The periods during which he operates to his own self-absorbed agenda sometimes lead to rifts with people. Those with Michael Owen and Alan Shearer had been for disparate professional and personal reasons.

'He falls out with people,' says Keegan's autobiography co-writer, Bob Harris. 'He has lost so many friends. It's not a word I want to use but I keep coming back to it . . . it's because he's selfish.

'He was never selfish around his parents, or his wife and children, or certain people close to him like Arthur Cox and Terry McDermott, but there are an awful lot he has left trailing in his wake. I think it's because he's focussed, blinkered.'

Terry McDermott, incidentally, once noticed that Keegan has a habit of addressing people as 'pal' when he is upset with them. Had Harris known that? 'Oh yes.'

This has echoes of something that Lee Clayton wrote in the *Daily Mail* of that time he spent ghosting Keegan's column for the *Sun*. Clayton found out about Keegan's first appointment as Newcastle manager via teletext. 'He later apologised by telephone for not sharing the news but our relationship was fractured and has never been restored. Being close to Keegan turned out to be just like his brand of football; great fun but nothing to show at the end of it . . . When he lets you down, it's a long way to fall.'

Everyone hung on to Keegan's words in those heady days after his first appointment to St James', when his name was familiar to players he would be recruiting and who admired and were even in awe of him. Now there was a new generation who had barely heard of him. David Ginola, Ali Benarbia and Nicolas Anelka had had their day.

It was something noticed by his old player Les Ferdinand, who had himself once been awestruck by Keegan. 'Over the summer you thought that things were going to happen, but then you start hearing rumours that he's not going to be able to buy the players he wants,' he said. 'He definitely needs to spend. But one of the problems he faces is that when I signed for him he was a big attraction for me to join Newcastle. Do players nowadays remember Kevin Keegan? Is he such a pull as he used to be as a manager?'

Now it would be money that would get the better among them to Tyneside – money and playing Champions League football. But both looked remote. The goalposts were continually moving at St James', it seemed, and Newcastle struggled to recruit. Back in March Terry McDermott had said: 'The calibre of player we are looking for, it will excite this club when it does happen. Once we have sorted out this season, you will see a big, big change at this club in its mentality and its players.'

The talk in the spring had been of Thierry Henry, Ronaldinho and even David Beckham. What actually happened was distinctly underwhelming. Some were shipped out, including the Czech centre-back David Rozenahl, who went to Lazio, and the Turkish midfield player Emre, who went to Fenerbahce. Their prices, £1.5million and £4million respectively, were about half of what Newcastle had paid for them.

By August the only arrivals at Newcastle were a young midfield player, Danny Guthrie, for a reported £1million from Liverpool, and an Argentine winger, Jonas Guttierez from Real Mallorca, for whom they paid £5million. For a while, Gutierrez was in dispute with his Spanish club about money owed and until this was settled Newcastle could not register him. At least they kept cornerstone defender Steve Taylor by improving his contract.

But sights were lower, and Keegan was being denied the money and the signings he wanted. 'Looking from the outside, it doesn't look good at all,' a source close to Keegan told me at the time. 'I'd love to know who's buying the players. I'm not sure he is. From what I hear, he doesn't know what players he is getting. They are being introduced.'

It was something Keegan hinted at in that radio interview with David Davies. Asked about a new contract for Michael Owen, he replied: 'I'm not involved in that, the way the club is organised. That's for Dennis Wise and Tony Jimenez to do.' Once, Keegan's lack of involvement would have been unthinkable.

Keegan desperately tried to sound upbeat in the interview – praising Ashley, talking about how well the club was structured and had moved on since his first spell, was geared to further progress – yet there was a sense that he was reining himself in after being held to account for public comments at the end of the previous season.

It was at that time that it was reported that Keegan and Terry McDermott had been to France to watch a player in a match for St Etienne against Paris St Germain; Wise and Jimenez had also attended the game but Keegan and McDermott had sat well apart from them. It seemed that left and right hand were not always communicating and had different responsibilities.

The summer was not therefore as busy for Keegan as he would have wanted. There was a smiling day when he went to Newcastle Airport to attend the photo opportunity of a Flybe aeroplane being named after him. Overshadowing it all, however, was the terrible tragedy of his brother Michael's son Craig being found dead in a Doncaster hotel room, believed to have suffered a drugs overdose.

When Keegan returned with the team for the first friendly, at Hartlepool, he took the chance to plead for more movement in the transfer market, insisting that he needed 'four quality signings' before the start of the season. Make your mind up, Mike Ashley might have said: only a few months previously Keegan had on various occasions said that the squad needed an overhaul, then that he would just need one or two new players. 'Ideally I'd like about twenty new players,' Keegan added in what seemed to be only a half-joking manner.

He repeated the need for new players, notably two new full-backs, the following week. This was after he had taken Newcastle to his hometown, Doncaster – now in their new Keepmoat Stadium – where Newcastle lost 1–0. It was still all quiet on the transfer front. Matters were not helped with injuries keeping Owen and Viduka out of most of the pre-season, while Obafemi Martins was given permission to return home to Nigeria after the death of his mother.

By now Ashley was apparently considering his own position at the club. A story appeared that an American finance company had offered him £320million for the club but that they backed off when he asked for £420million. Actually, the company said, they had been approached but were not interested. Then came a tale that Tony Jimenez had been dispatched to Dubai to see if Dubai International Capital, potential buyers of Liverpool, were interested in investing. They weren't.

Eventually Ashley had to deny a story that he had been in buy-out talks with a branch of the family of Osama Bin Laden – they ran a construction company and had long since distanced themselves from him. Ashley could not deny, however, that he was seeking a financial injection.

'Genuinely, genuinely I am not looking for Newcastle shareholders in a cave in Afghanistan,' he joked gauchely to financial journalists. 'Good morning, Bin. How are you in your cave in Afghanistan? Would you like to come and sit next to me at the Toon army? Clearly not. Is that a rucksack you've got with you? Oh good.' (Ashley had possibly not heard that Bin Laden had once been a watcher of Arsenal, anyway, during a time spent in London.)

Ashley added that he was willing to sell 'a portion' of the club, since he was sitting, he said, in a very expensive seat. There were also personal finances to consider. Newcastle had been losing money and continued to under him, eating into that near-£1billion fortune from the flotation of his company, Sports Direct. He was also looking at a paper loss of more than £200million after placing a massive bet that the share price of the HBoS bank would rise.

In addition, Sports Direct was not trading well and city investors who had bought into his flotation did not like the way the company was doing business. Profits were expected to fall from £104million to £97million. It accounted for the belt-tightening. How sadly apt it seemed that the fall of Newcastle's sponsors Northern Rock had brought into focus the whole issue of Britain falling into recession.

There was constant scrutiny of Keegan's relationship with Ashley – uneasy as it seemed, uneasy as it at times made Keegan feel. Ashley was said to have previously been virtually reclusive, a man who hated the public gaze. Business journalists seemed astonished at the way he now stepped into the limelight. You wondered quite what image Ashley thought he was projecting by wearing replica shirts all the time. Would top, sophisticated players want to come to a club where the owner was clad in a home shirt that stretched those black-and-white stripes to their limit?

There were tales of behaviour, too, that left rival clubs distinctly unimpressed. When the Newcastle directors went to West Ham for example, there was no sign of Ashley pre-match, which upset the home board since they had been asked for extra tickets to accommodate Ashley's companions. At the end of the game Ashley did turn up, in replica shirt with a coterie of hangers-on. All wanted pints of draught lager, which the Upton Park boardroom does not stock, and a waitress had to be dispatched to another lounge.

At St James' Park, Sunderland directors were also unimpressed by Ashley and his friends arriving in the boardroom at the end of the match punching the air and crowing about their victory in the manner of fans rather than club officials.

Keegan was clearly keeping his options open, may even have been using the job to further his Soccer Circus cause. With the focus on him as Newcastle struggled early in his tenure, he returned to Glasgow to check on his business, happy to have the cameras and journalists there to record it all. He opened another facility at a new Center Parcs holiday complex in Cumbria and then announced plans for more Soccer Circus outlets in China and Dubai.

Just before the season started, things looked up when Keegan took delivery of a new centre-back, for a fee believed to be around £5million, from Deportivo La Coruna. The

Argentine Fabricio Coloccini certainly looked the part, as did the industrious Gutierrez, as Newcastle began the season with a creditable 1–1 draw against Manchester United at Old Trafford.

The following week, Michael Owen came off the bench to grab the winning goal against Bolton Wanderers to give them a promising start of four points from two games. When they then went to Coventry City and won 3–2 in the Carling Cup, with James Milner outstanding, it looked as if they might be ready to surprise a few people.

Despite all the intrigue around Newcastle United, Kevin Keegan and Mike Ashley, there did seem to be one outcome that people were not contemplating. And that was Keegan staying and succeeding. Could the big river indeed rise again?

A 3–0 defeat at Arsenal, mirroring the two towards the end of the previous season, was no great surprise and Keegan remained upbeat in his press conference afterwards. The questions centred more on his introduction of Joey Barton as a substitute – he would receive a twelve-match ban, with six games suspended, from the FA a week later as a result of the Ousmane Dabo incident – and a tackle by the player on Samir Nasri. The little Frenchman retaliated with a kick at Barton, which enraged Keegan, who had words with Nasri at the final whistle.

When it came to new players, Keegan was staying optimistic, publicly at least. It had been his decision, he had emphasised before the game, to sell James Milner to Aston

Villa for £12million during the week. Now he said that judgement should be reserved until after Monday's transfer deadline day, the first day of September. He expected some good-quality reinforcements to be arriving. He was keeping his powder dry, his misgivings to himself, as he had done a couple of weeks earlier when his ever-faithful ally Arthur Cox quietly left the club in a move dispiriting to him and more significant than it appeared at the time.

When Monday turned into Tuesday, however, all hell broke loose.

Keegan had hoped that the Milner money would enable him to buy players he wanted. Instead, he was told that Dennis Wise and Tony Jimenez were bringing in a striker from Deportivo La Coruna for £5million by the moniker of Xisco and a Uruguayan midfield player named Ignacio Gonzalez on loan for the season from Valencia.

The manager reportedly said that he had never heard of them. He was apparently told to go and check out the players on YouTube. Keegan was furious to discover, too, that his entire first-team squad had been put up for sale on the Monday, with clubs being faxed details of, particularly, the high earners Barton and Owen, but there were no takers.

In meetings chaired by Derek Llambias, Keegan asked forcefully what was going on. He was reminded of the club's structure these days, and a policy of recruiting younger players from abroad along the Arsene Wenger lines at Arsenal – Xisco was a Spanish Under-21 international, on cheaper wages and with a potentially higher resale value. Keegan asserted his belief that he was supposed to be the one who sanctioned signings and that these were not up to his standards.

Keegan departed with the club believing he had resigned, though various news outlets keeping a vigil outside St James' Park in front of knots of fans chanting 'Sack the board' were reporting that he had been sacked. As the affair rumbled on for two days, the two parties gave the impression of trying to patch things up, with the new chief executive of the League Managers' Association, Richard Bevan, as mediator but it was no good.

When Keegan heard that Ashley was in New York – he would be photographed that week dancing on tables in the Pink Elephant bar as his party racked up a bill of $200,000 – and would not be returning for talks, the game was up. The marriage of convenience, that had turned into a marriage from hell, was over after just eight months. At first numb, Newcastle's support grew ever angrier at their club becoming a laughing stock again.

Once more, as he has always done in these situations, Keegan went to ground, Richard Bevan becoming his spokesman. Keegan's position had been undermined by signings imposed on him, Bevan said. The acrimony continued when Newcastle issued a statement saying Keegan had known the situation at the club all along and agreed to his role in matters.

Wherever the truth lay, it was going to be left now to lawyers to sort out the divorce settlement. Keegan's resignation may have been surprising, given his need to earn again and recover some losses from Soccer Circus, but he clearly felt he had a case for constructive dismissal and a big financial settlement. Newcastle, for their part, believed that Keegan owed them £2million. They were letting it be known that, well aware of his history, they had inserted the compensation clause in the contract should he walk out.

They would have to do a bit better than that. Keegan would emerge again as the hero. Ashley, who had been caught by TV cameras at Arsenal downing a pint of lager in one to further his oafish image, was the villain, along with the motley cast of characters he had assembled as his lieutenants. What was that Jack Charlton line about Keegan? About him jumping into the Tyne and coming up with a salmon?

Tyneside turned on Ashley and his 'Cockney Mafia' and the owner, fed up with the criticism and perceived ingratitude, put the club up for sale. Through Wise and Jimenez, he sought an interim manager who might restore the club's credibility for any prospective purchaser.

The irony was that the headhunters, who had been charged with finding fresh young players, could only come up with the names of old hands they had worked with. Glenn Hoddle, even Dave Bassett, were linked with the job. Terry Venables wanted assurances beyond a reported £100,000 a match, that he would be given time and scope to do the job properly. Then, out of left field, the old Wimbledon manager Joe Kinnear got the call to be the caretaker manager to confirm what a shambles it had all become.

As for buyers, the Indian businessman Anil Ambani was linked as the Premier League contracted billionaireitis in the wake of Dr Sulaiman Al Fahim taking over Manchester City, but he declined. A Nigerian consortium was mooted, the attraction for Newcastle fans coming in the form of word that they might reinstate Keegan.

This time around, Keegan had looked out of his time, however; certainly in the wrong place with the wrong people though he had always seen Newcastle as his spiritual home. The money men now involved in the Premier League – at least those at the less successful clubs – wanted bigger bangs and a bigger say in playing matters for their bucks. The days of a manager having complete control of budgets and signings, in the way that Lawrie McMenemy had when he signed Keegan for Southampton, looked numbered.

Dewy-eyed notions that Keegan may have had of reprising his first Newcastle reign, of buying and selling and being left to get on with it as he enjoyed the reverence of both his board and fans, were simply fanciful when confronted by hard-nosed men like Mike Ashley.

Given how it ended, it is fascinating, in hindsight, to recall some of the comments of those I consulted on Keegan before his exit.

'He's come back and he knows it's his last job, unless he buys a club or something, because he will never be a director of football,' said Mark Lawrenson. 'He's got to give this a real go. He's not daft.

'But you know one day he'll walk in and say to Mike Ashley, "Thanks very much." As a manager, you have got to be able to pick your own players and it's not going to happen, from what I hear.'

And Sir Bobby Robson said to me in the summer: 'I think Keegan will retire in three years. I think he will see his stint out but I don't think he will go on. I think he is in for the long haul – unless it all goes horribly wrong, unless they won't give him the money and make it difficult for him so that he can't sign players or change the way they play rapidly.'

Then it could happen, as David Davies sums up. 'I think he has spells when he falls out of love with football, not with the game itself but all the paraphernalia that goes with a sport like football, the world game, the beautiful or not so beautiful game.'

Given Sir Bobby's belief that Keegan still had some years left in him, and having got over the disillusion that Davies perceives, could it mean that Keegan has another job in him, should someone still see merit in that brand of open-hearted, old-fashioned motivational management?

'I do think his approach can still work,' Lawrenson says. 'Even more these days you've got to be players' mates, haven't you? I think Kevin is very good at that.' Avram Grant had said something similar during his Chelsea side's run-in to the title with Manchester United the previous season: that Sir Alex Ferguson has changed down the years and become more friendly with his players. The old dictatorial ways no longer work with millionaires.

And Keegan does have a great determination to prove people wrong, to overcome the doubts of the gainsayers. David Ginola offers a fascinating insight into the stickability which is at odds with the view of him as a quitter.

'I was beating him at Turnberry, the lighthouse, the golf,' he says. 'We were at hole number fourteen and it was raining, a stormy day. You couldn't even put the golf umbrellas up, it was so windy. I was winning so I say, "OK, we shake hands now, we go back to the clubhouse and have a nice cup of tea." I was saying, "Please gaffer, can we go back?" The ball was going all over the place.

'He got really angry, saying he wasn't going to let a Frenchman beat him. So I said, "OK, let's carry on." All the players had gone back to the clubhouse. It was just me and him by then. No way was he going to stop. He was the winner in the end. I lost on the eighteenth.'

There was hope in all the professionals who speak of Keegan, have known him well and retain a reservoir of goodwill for him, that he could end his career on a high note rather than in anticlimax. They have known an effervescent character, one who has fought his whole life to shake off his lowly born status – however proud of it and motivating it has been for him – and one who has always survived and bounced back into the spotlight after recovering his resilience. Latterly, though, there did seem to be something less dynamic about him.

He seemed more sensitive, certainly to criticism, and more

easily hurt. Indeed there appeared a gloom even, a sadness about the fact that he was being forced to mind his Ps and Qs, to tolerate the wrist-slapping, and allowed himself to be overlooked and overruled in certain decision-making, where once he was decision-maker.

'He is a different Kevin Keegan to the one who signed me,' Les Ferdinand told the *Mail on Sunday*. 'He was a bit more effervescent back then.

'I was there on the day of his first match back. It was a five-thirty p.m. start and he was in there two and a half hours before the game. He, Terry McDermott and myself were reminiscing and he was bubbly and bright. Everything was like the Keegan of old. But over a period of weeks I slowly saw that drain out of him.'

The game of football nourishes and drains, gives and takes, enriches and appals. It is both gift and curse. Keegan has seen it all, has desperately sought to retain his optimism and enthusiasm but has frequently found himself disillusioned. He has brought much to the game over the last forty years, as player and manager, pundit and character.

'Problems,' he once said, 'are just opportunities in work clothes.' You wonder if those clothes fit snugly any more. The sport is more clinical, less spontaneous now. You wonder if even Keegan believes that he can recapture the joy; whether or not the fantasy and romanticism he brought – flawed, like himself, as it was – is for another era. However big, indeed inflated, the Premier League seems these days, there is sometimes the sense of its smallness of spirit.

In Billy Wilder's brilliant 1950 black-and-white film *Sunset Boulevard*, a desperate writer by the name of Joe Gillis is trying to evade people to whom he owes money. He eventually seeks sanctuary in the shabby, grand old house of a fading screen idol by the name of Norma Desmond.

'You used to be in silent pictures,' he says. 'You used to be big.'

'I am big,' she replies. 'It's the pictures that got small.'

INDEX

ABOUT THE AUTHOR

Ian Ridley, voted Sports Journalist of the Year in the British Press Awards 2007, is Football Columnist for the *Mail on Sunday*. He is the co-author of Tony Adams's autobiography *Addicted* and also wrote *Floodlit Dreams*, his account of life as a football club chairman.